# from
# CHAOS
## to CARE

# David Lawrence, M.D.

Chairman Emeritus, Kaiser Permanente

# from
# CHAOS
# to CARE

the promise of
**TEAM-BASED MEDICINE**

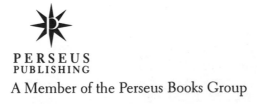

**PERSEUS**
PUBLISHING
A Member of the Perseus Books Group

Cataloging-in-Publication Data is available from the Library of Congress
ISBN 0–7382–0753–5

Perseus Publishing is a member of the Perseus Books Group.
Find us on the World Wide Web at http://www.perseuspublishing.com.

Perseus Publishing books are available at special discounts for bulk purchases in the U.S. by corporations, institutions, and other organizations. For more information, please contact the Special Markets Department at the Perseus Books Group, 11 Cambridge Center, Cambridge, MA 02142, or call (800) 255-1514 or (617) 252-5298, or e-mail j.mccrary@perseusbooks.com.

Text design by *Reginald Thompson*
Set in 11-point Sabon by the Perseus Books Group

First printing, October 2002

1 2 3 4 5 6 7 8 9 10—04 03 02

*Paul Eckley,*
*who lit the flame;*

*Kurt Deuschle,*
*who kept it burning when it was young;*

*Amos Lawrence,*
*who supported it for a shared lifetime.*

# CONTENTS

# A NOTE TO THE READER

SEVERAL CONCESSIONS HAVE been made in this book to make it flow more easily and to avoid troublesome jargon and tiring specificity.

Throughout the book, with some exceptions that are obvious, I have used *the patient* to refer to a constellation of people including the patient, the family, and other associated friends and neighbors who become involved in the caregiving process. The problems with that tangle are clear.

*Physicians* are distinguished from other *medical professionals* because of their central role in the delivery of medical care. By *medical professional*, I mean any medically trained person other than a doctor whose expertise helps the patient: nurse, nurse practitioner, physician assistant, pharmacist, health educator, nutritionist, social worker, and any of a host of other professionals involved in direct patient care. *Support workers* help the physicians and medical professionals carry out their work. Occasionally, the reader will see that physicians and medical professionals are lumped together as *providers,* a word many physicians loathe. I do so not to aggravate them but to make life easier for the reader.

The tiresome debate about *health care* versus *medical care* never ends. Although there are useful distinctions between the two, they are relatively obscure. I have ignored them, referring to the whole kit and caboodle as *medical care.*

The term *medical-care delivery system* is unfortunate but necessary jargon to cover all of the professionals engaged in caring for patients, the support workers who make it possible for the professionals to do their work, and the institutions and support services that medical care involves. The delivery system does not include the payment system or the medical-insurance system. Both are important, but they are different matters that I have dealt with only as they affect the delivery system in the context of this book.

I often refer to *chronic* or *complex* illnesses. The distinction is this: Chronic illnesses are conditions lasting more than three months, whereas complex illnesses are serious conditions requiring major medical interventions—surgical and medical—but where the patient returns to nearly normal functioning within the three-month time frame. Diabetes, heart disease, asthma, cancer, genetic abnormalities, and the like are examples of the former. Trauma, acute appendicitis, and severe but treatable infections are examples of the latter.

The politically and factually correct "his and hers" and "he and she" has given way to the male gender to ease the task for the reader. I apologize to the medical-care workforce in the country, the majority of whom are women.

Two important devices are used to call attention to issues highlighted in this book. First, I have used the example of a fictional asthma patient, a child named Rebecca. A patient with some other chronic illness could have served just as well. Asthma was selected because the care issues are clear and dramatic, and because the burdens placed on the family by this chronic illness are easily described.

Second, I have described a Dr. Landers, a hypothetical solo general pediatrician. One might argue that Landers is a straw man, as it is more common for general pediatricians to practice in small, single-specialty groups of three to ten physicians than alone. I believe the challenges facing practicing physicians today, regardless of specialty, are no more easily addressed in these small groups than among solo practitioners. The Landers story makes it easier to underscore the difficulties.

Some may quibble with Landers's workload and practice organization. I have made no effort to create an "average" general pediatrician in either sense; instead Landers falls within the broad range of workloads and practice choices that one finds among general pediatricians. I urge the reader to look past specific details to the issues that Landers and his physician colleagues must deal with today.

# INTRODUCTION

MY FATHER DIED in November 1999, six months before his ninetieth birthday. He'd been failing for several years, but his final decline began suddenly. One afternoon, standing outside the home he'd shared for twenty years with his wife, his heart began to beat irregularly. Decreased blood flow to his brain caused him to lose consciousness, fall, and break his hip. Dazed and in pain, he was transported by ambulance to an excellent local community hospital. Following the recommendations of his longtime primary-care physician and a bone specialist, he chose to have his hip repaired. He was counting on several more years of active living and didn't want to be confined to a walker or wheelchair. For two days his recovery was uneventful. Then he inhaled food while eating, developed pneumonia, and stopped breathing. A lung specialist put in an emergency breathing tube, and a digestive-tract specialist put in a feeding tube through his stomach wall because he no longer could swallow safely. For several days he lay between life and death in the intensive care unit, in and out of consciousness, often confused. Eventually he recovered enough to be moved to a local rehabilitation hospital, where he received therapy to help him use a walker and speak more clearly. During the twenty-eight-day stay covered by Medicare, he progressed slowly and regained some strength. From there he was transferred to a nursing home selected because it had a decent reputation and was close enough for his wife to visit each day.

He went downhill almost immediately after he was moved. When blood was found in his stool, the nurses and resident doctor sent him to another specialist without notifying anyone in the family or consulting with his primary physician. Extensive examination revealed an advanced cancer of the lower bowel. The specialist wanted to tell Dad right away, but we persuaded him to wait until we had a chance to talk among ourselves and explore hospice services in the community. When his wife shared the results with him, he accepted the diagnosis with equanimity and said he wanted time to think over his choices. Two days later he became confused and agitated, his breathing labored. Within several hours he died of pneumonia.

I had been his physician-counselor-son, talking with his doctors, checking out treatment alternatives for his various ailments, working with him to decide about home care when he could no longer manage his medications and personal hygiene to his satisfaction. He lived across the country in the small city where I'd attended medical school. In spite of the distance, I usually could find out what he needed through classmates practicing in the community.

In those last weeks before his death, though, I was unprepared for how hard it was to get the information I needed to help him make decisions about his treatment and care arrangements. Being a local medical-school graduate and an executive in a large medical organization didn't help. I was just a son, joining my brother and sister and father's wife to help our father navigate a medical-care system ill-suited to deliver what he required.

The professionals who cared for Dad weren't incompetent or unfeeling. In fact, almost everyone was well trained and well intended. They cared about their work and seemed to care about him. Many took time to get to know him, at least a little, often sharing with us something he'd said that made them laugh together. Most worked long hours and tried to help us deal with the decisions we faced. Individual clinical judgments seemed appropriate.

All of them, though—doctors, nurses, and the many other professionals and support staff—seemed harried and over-worked. We had trouble getting through to them even when I used my doctor title. Information moved slowly and irregularly from one doctor to another or from doctor to nurse, when it moved at all. Conflicting diagnoses and recommendations con-fused us and delayed treatment decisions. Nurses at the nursing home were unable to arrange a time to meet with the primary-care physician to map a course of action once my father was transferred from the rehab hospital. No useful information was available to help us decide which doctors or facilities to go to for the best care; we relied instead on anecdotes and recom-mendations from friends. When Dad's primary-care physician retired, he referred Dad to another doctor. We had no idea who this person was, whether or not he was competent, how he dealt with elderly patients, or what his approach to terminal care might be.

Stories haunt me. The day-nurse in the rehabilitation hospi-tal slumped in her chair at the end of her shift, gray with fatigue, rubbed her eyes slowly, and softly complained about the daily balancing act she performed between spending time with pa-tients, whom she loves, and doing the paperwork, which she loathes. In a low monotone to make sure he didn't interrupt my father's nap, a young physician spewed frustration and anger about medicine, imploring me to explain what to expect from his chosen profession in the future. Dad's wife agonized about whether or not to cancel three of his medical appointments scheduled on successive days in different parts of the city. She would have to pick him up at the nursing home, load him into the car by herself, drive to each location, wheel him into the doc-tor's office, accompany him in the exam room, and return him to the nursing home. She couldn't sleep and ate fitfully, trying to ignore the irregular racing of her heart that left her weak and out of breath.

Throughout Dad's illness, I separated the experiences we had with his care from the professional work I was part of at that time. The challenge of getting information, understanding the choices, and making sure Dad and his wife were cared for took every ounce of energy my brother and sister and I had. There wasn't time to think about why this was happening or how to make it better. At least not until he died.

After the funeral was over and my life found its new rhythm without the phone calls or weekly visits that had connected Dad and me for many years, I remembered his tears of outrage when he told me how he'd hung out of his bed in the ICU, secured by his wrists and ankles to keep him from pulling out his stomach tube and his blood lines when he was confused at night. He had soiled himself suspended there before a nurse found him. I remembered the nurse from the nursing home who called my office 2,000 miles away to ask me to authorize the staff to feed Dad something by mouth instead of through his feeding tube. Her insensitive explanation that "the Old Boy deserves some pleasure because he's going to die soon from his cancer" left me speechless. I remembered how doctors couldn't get information from other doctors, or appointments conflicted, or medications that one doctor prescribed interfered with those another doctor ordered, and I saw firsthand why so many people describe their medical care as a "nightmare to navigate." I remembered how we struggled to deal with Dad's care; how we watched him suffer and die; how helpless we felt because no matter what we tried, we couldn't make him well again or make his care better for him.

Only then did my professional work merge with those personal experiences. I have been involved in direct patient care either as a clinician or as a manager for most of my career. For the past two decades, I have been a part of Kaiser Permanente, the nation's largest integrated medical-care system and a leader in developing more effective ways to care for patients. Starting in the mid-1990s, I joined two national efforts to better understand the problems of poor quality and safety in American medicine. The first occurred over three years in gatherings that brought together a small group of medical leaders from around the country at the Kennedy School at Harvard University. The second was a several-year study sponsored by the Institute of Medicine of the National Academy of Sciences. We immersed ourselves in the literature about medical quality and patient safety, the debate about why the problems were so pervasive and intractable, and the difficult process of determining how to resolve them. Dad died the same year that the Institute of Medicine published the widely publicized report *To Err Is Human,* in which we described the problems of errors in American medicine and provided recommendations about how to improve safety. One year earlier, the institute had published the results of our study documenting pervasive problems in medical quality across the country, *The Quality of Care in America* report. The last in the series, *Crossing the Quality Chasm,* appeared in March 2001. In it we offered an explanation of why these problems occur and what could be done to change the medical-care system for the better.

Once our family had time to say goodbye to Dad and the miserable details of death were behind us, I realized that the policy abstractions of the institute studies and the Harvard conversations had new meaning. The problems that we documented now had a human face. And the lessons from Kaiser Permanente and other innovative medical-care systems both large and small could provide important insights for how we might better respond.

I've written this book to share the studies, the dialogues, and the abstractions in order to explore what is going on, why, and what we can do to change it. The work of the institute and many others is a starting point, and exciting examples of innovations demonstrate how medical care can be provided well and affordably. Many of the pieces that we need to create an outstanding and affordable medical-care system are already in place. But they are scattered, disjointed, isolated from one another, fragments of a vast and costly puzzle that is still missing critical pieces. Medical care is like the chaos in an ant colony that occurs immediately after the nest is stirred with a stick. Our challenge is to leave that chaos behind, to identify innovations that work, and to knit the pieces together into something that works for patients across the nation.

Anger provides energy for this task. I accept my father's death. His was a full, complete life, and he died loved and loving. But with all we know about good, safe, and responsive care, with all our nation spends on health care, he shouldn't have suffered as he did. He shouldn't have been as confused about his care as he was, and he shouldn't have experienced the indignities he did. It was too hard for him and his family. We can do much better.

But anger isn't the only motivation for writing this book. I love my profession. Doctors and the professionals who work with us share the privilege of joining the promise of medical science and technology with care and caring. At its best, medicine is remarkable. But when we fail or harm our patients, it is agonizing. When we neglect to address the problems of quality, safety, responsiveness, and waste that bring our nation's medical bill and the number of people without medical insurance to the highest in the developed world, it is damning because solutions are so close at hand. When the knowledge and tools that are the product of our nation's investments in medical science and technology do not reach patients who can benefit from them, it is inexcusable. And when these failures occur because of our resistance to change, it is intolerable.

Fortunately, we find examples scattered throughout the country where up-to-date science, not shopworn habit, is the basis for clinical decisions, where learning is constant and purposeful, and where errors are discovered early and prevented. Patients are the center of care rather than bystanders on whom medicine is practiced. Professionals and patients work together to decide on a treatment plan, and medical care is coordinated and integrated for the benefit of each patient. In these places, the human and economic toll of poor care has been markedly reduced.

These islands are beacons, our hope. They are not yet connected to the medical mainland, however. Efforts to do so provoke a fierce response as those in the mainstream protect an outdated way of practice and a form of professionalism that no longer serves the interests of those who need care or those who pay for it.

My intent in this book is to extract the lessons these examples provide and build on them to describe a care system that meets the six aims outlined in the Institute of Medicine study *Crossing the Quality Chasm*: medical care that is consistently effective, safe, responsive, timely, affordable, and equitable. To get there, I have outlined actions that must be taken by those who play the greatest role in shaping medicine's future and overcoming resistance to change: purchasers, insurers, government, and patients, as well as those whose innovations continue to light the way.

In the chapters that follow, I have joined emotion and abstraction in discussion and story. At the center are the challenges that medicine confronts and the changes required to respond. Intertwined is the fictional story of Rebecca, a young child with severe asthma, as told by her mother. We also examine the practice of Rebecca's first physician, Dr. Adam Landers, a pediatrician in solo practice. The formal sections provide the description of a system that can provide the medical care we seek and need. The story of Rebecca and her family, and Dr. Landers, illustrates how care can change for the better when a patient moves out of the chaos so common today to medical care designed to join the remarkable tools that modern science and technology have given us with the caring so important to our healing.

The people—Rebecca, her family, Dr. Landers, and the other patients mentioned by name—are not real, although their stories are typical. I have tried to protect the privacy of those patients who shared their experiences with me, while honoring the spirit in which they offered them.

Medicine, at its best, gives us health and hope that was unimaginable a few decades ago. It can help us relieve our suffering and reclaim our lives when we are ill and provide tools to prevent disease and maintain our health when we are well. My father's experience is a warning, though, that echoes in experiences too many share. The echo will continue on and on, through the doctors' offices and clinics, hospitals and nursing homes, laboratories and pharmacies of twenty-first-century medical care, until this chaotic medical Humpty Dumpty can be pieced together into care that works for us.

# from
# CHAOS
## to CARE

# 1

# REBECCA, AGES TWO TO SIX: THE CHAOTIC YEARS WITH DR. LANDERS

*The following fictional account is told from the perspective of the mother of Rebecca, a young asthma patient, as the family navigates a medical-care system that lacks a team-based approach.*

THE NEWSPAPER MUST have startled me when it hit the front door. I could hear the delivery van drive on up the street; its tires hissed on the rainy pavement, newspapers slid along the sidewalks and thumped into doors. Whenever I sleep in the chair, even for a couple of hours like last night, my neck hurts and my left leg goes numb. What was this, the third night in a row? The night before that, I know, was the emergency room. All night and an hour's sleep on the bench in the waiting room. When was the last time I slept through the night in my own bed? It must have been last week, when John took care of Rebecca.

She's lost in her bed, she's so small. But she's breathing more easily now. There's sweat on her upper lip and she's still fighting that cold, though. I hate the sounds she makes. She wheezes when she breathes in, then grunts when she pushes the air out. I can feel buzzing like sandpaper when I put my hand on her chest. It's so hard for her when she has these attacks.

John left early. He's got a big case going to trial next month and has been working on it night and day. When he sleeps in the chair he looks gray in the morning. So do I, I guess. Neither of us gets enough sleep. I'll call Yoshi to ask if she can handle the shop again. She's getting tired of covering for me. We didn't plan it this way when we opened our shop. Each of us was going to work two days a week, close on Mondays, and both be in the shop on Saturday. But ever since Rebecca got sick, Yoshi's been filling in at least one day a week. She doesn't complain because she knows I haven't got a choice: doctor visits, nights in the ER, too tired to handle the cash register, snapping at our customers. It isn't fair to her.

I hope Jenny does okay on her arithmetic test today. She's struggling. I never seem to have the energy to help her with her homework. Neither does John. We try. I just don't have the patience for it lots of nights anymore, especially when I've been up most of the night with Rebecca.

I've got to get an appointment with Dr. Landers today. That higher dose of medicine he prescribed is making Rebecca sick to her stomach. How many times has it been? Five visits to the ER in the past two months? It's always worse in the winter and spring. And of course the attacks always happen in the middle of the night, after the other kids are asleep.

I forgot. Today's Dr. Landers's day off, so we'll go tomorrow. Rebecca can't go to school today, and she'll be out most of tomorrow, too. I hope they don't hold her back in first grade for next year, but then, I could see why they would. I can't remember the last time she was in class for two weeks straight without being home at least a day or two. Her teachers tell me she keeps to herself, doesn't talk, doesn't play like the others either. She always gets sick when she tries to do what the other kids do. That Bumblebee soccer thing was horrible. At the first practice, the coaches made her run up and down the field a couple of times, and when she started wheezing, Bill Sandoval, the assistant coach, panicked and brought her straight home to us. John and I couldn't stop the attack, so John took her to the emergency room.

She'd just turned two when she had her first attack. She always was a fussy eater, and she had colds all the time. But Dr. Landers told us not to worry. Michael and Jen weren't sick very often. When they were, Dr. Landers was really good with them. He made us feel better, too. John and I have a lot of confidence in him. So when he told us Rebecca would outgrow the colds and fussiness, we felt better.

That night was awful! She didn't want to sleep. I sang to her and rubbed her back, but she was really restless. She cried when I tried to leave the room. She was wheezing a little, but I thought it was her cold. Finally she dozed off, and I was able to read to Michael and Jen. Just about the time John and I were ready to go to bed, we heard horrible sounds coming from Rebecca's room.

She was sitting in her crib, her chest heaving up and down, her lips blue, her eyes wide, scared to death. She was gasping for air, breathing so fast. The cords in her neck were like ropes holding a tent in the wind. Each time she breathed in there were horrible sounds: pops, whistles, rasping, phlegm caught in her chest. She seemed to bite the air into her mouth she struggled so hard. Then she grunted and pushed the air out, and it took forever. In and out, in and out, her chest blown up, the sweat pouring down her face, her hair wet. She'd cough until I thought she'd never breathe again. All the while, she looked at me, frightened, too tired even to reach for me. I was so scared she'd die!

When the ambulance got here, the attendants took one look at her, started an IV, and loaded her into the ambulance right away. I went with her to the emergency room at North City Hospital, holding her on the bed. John asked Willa Nickleson, our next-door neighbor, to come over and stay with the kids. They were awake and crying.

The doctors in emergency were good with Rebecca. They knew exactly what to do. They put some more medication into her IV that helped her breathe. And they had her breathe from a machine to get her some more medication. After blood was taken and the chest X ray was finished, we held her hands and rubbed her legs and chest, and pretty soon she calmed down enough to sleep. Her breathing didn't get back to normal for several hours, though, and the doctors wouldn't discharge her until those buzzing and whistling sounds were gone. The X rays showed how pumped up her lungs were when she first came in, and they were kind of fuzzy. By the time she left, her lungs were more relaxed and clearer. I got used to seeing those X rays. After a year or two, I could show the doctors what the differences were because they took X rays every time we came in.

A pediatrician who shares call with Dr. Landers came by to check on us when he got to the hospital in the morning. He told us that Rebecca had suffered an asthma attack, a relatively common problem with children that they often outgrow. Medications can control the disease in the meantime, he said, and he promised to let Dr. Landers know what happened. The emergency doctor wrote out several prescriptions for Rebecca. By the time we had them filled at the drugstore, it had been nearly twenty-four hours since we'd left in the ambulance.

Anne from Dr. Landers's office called the next morning to schedule an appointment for later in the day. Dr. Landers was great. He asked questions about how Rebecca had been feeling before the attack, what she'd eaten, how she'd slept. He examined her, and when he listened to her lungs, he let me hear the wheezes through his stethoscope. Dr. Landers agreed that she had asthma. He told us it was not uncommon in children, and that it could be controlled with the new drugs available. He took more blood samples, did another X ray, and sent us home with three prescriptions for Rebecca to take instead of the ones the emergency-room doctor had given us. One, he said, was an inhaler to use every day to control the inflammation. One was to relax the muscles of the breathing tubes. And another was to use if she started having symptoms of an attack. He asked us to pick up the "Managing Asthma" pamphlet in the waiting room.

We felt so confident after that first visit. We read the pamphlet, went over everything Dr. Landers told us, and made sure we read the instructions for the medications. We trusted and liked Dr. Landers, and knew that North City Hospital had a good reputation.

Initially Rebecca did pretty well. She slept through the night, and John and I were able to keep up our regular schedules. Then two months later, she had another attack, worse than the first. This one really shook us. Dr. Landers changed the doses of two of the medications and continued to reassure us that we didn't need to take Rebecca to a specialist. After that I lose track. We went from emergency room to Dr. Landers and back again. I think we were in the emergency room with Rebecca sometimes as often as twice a month. Nothing worked. Rebecca didn't get any better, and Dr. Landers tried everything, believe me.

When he referred us to an allergy specialist, our hopes rose again. The doctor was pretty businesslike, although Rebecca didn't like her very much because of the tests she did with scratches on Rebecca's arms. Oh, did Rebecca scream before we went to those visits! I had to hold her down to get her dressed sometimes, and then she'd wheeze and have trouble breathing, so I'd give her a couple of puffs on the inhaler to calm her down. We found out that Rebecca is allergic to several things, so the doctor began "desensitizing" her with regular injections. She also prescribed another medication on top of the ones we were already using. That whole process took twenty visits or so.

The allergist kept asking me what medications Rebecca was taking, because it always took a long time for her office assistant to get through to Dr. Landers's office. Twice when I took Rebecca to see Dr. Landers, he told me he didn't have the information from the allergist and would have to wait to decide what else to suggest until he talked with her. That's when John and I started to keep notes about the visits—what the doctors told us, what the prescriptions were. It was just too confusing to keep track of otherwise.

The allergist told us to get nonallergenic pillows and comforters for the whole family, since feathers can cause allergic reactions. She told us to get rid of our cats and dog, too. That was really hard because the children were so attached to the pets. We were also supposed to keep the house free of dust and molds, so we had to hire someone to clean the house each week.

In addition to the allergist, we've seen a lot of other doctors, too—probably ten or fifteen in all. Some Dr. Landers referred us to; others we went to for second opinions. We also got to know the doctors at the emergency room and in the hospital. That infectious-disease specialist Dr. Landers called in at the hospital when Rebecca had pneumonia the first time was really something: I think his name was Dr. Charles. He swept into the room with two or three young doctors in tow like some big shot and began to ask me all sorts of questions. When I told him that we'd answered the same ones for Dr. Landers, the doctors in the emergency room, the attending pediatrician in the intensive care unit, and Dr. Landers's associate, he told me that he never relies on what anyone else has done. "After all," he said, "you're paying me for my training and experience." He was pretty condescending, but after he found out John is a lawyer, he treated me like I might be halfway competent.

Dr. Charles didn't agree with Dr. Landers's treatment plan, so he changed Rebecca's antibiotics to something more specific for her problem, increased the concentration in her inhalants, added some other drug "to help her lungs clear," and rushed out. He saw Rebecca every day while she was in the intensive care unit, and then two or three more times when she was on the regular pediatric floor. Dr. Landers came by every day, too. He never contradicted Dr. Charles, although I did hear them arguing outside Rebecca's room one morning. After Rebecca was discharged from the hospital and we went back to Dr. Landers, he left her on one of the medications Dr. Charles had prescribed but switched her back to the doses she was on before she went into the hospital with the other ones. By that time, we were pretty confused.

Rebecca has only had to be admitted to the hospital three times since she got asthma. So we've been pretty lucky, but she really hates being in the hospital. We do, too, for that matter. The nurses and the staff are nice enough, but it's scary for her. Someone's always putting a needle in her or doing something that keeps her from sleeping. She always wants us to hold her. She doesn't cry quite so much anymore, though. Now she gets quiet, like she's watching everything from a distance, and I can tell she's scared. She almost died once in the hospital. She had a reaction to an antibiotic the infectious-disease doctor ordered. She started wheezing, coughing, struggling to breathe, and turning blue. Those noises when she can't breathe . . . Oh, God, it's awful! The nurse gave Rebecca an injection right away—adrenaline, I think—and then another. Rebecca settled down after fifteen minutes or so. The nurse explained that Rebecca was "pretty close." She made sure we wrote down the name of the antibiotic so that no one would prescribe it for Rebecca again.

I'm glad we did. About six months later, John took her to the emergency room again. When she was ready to come home, the emergency-room physician prescribed an antibiotic for her cold. Almost like an afterthought, he asked John if Rebecca was allergic to anything. John checked our notes and saw the entry I'd made about Rebecca's reaction. He pointed it out to the emergency-room doctor, who wrote out a different prescription. John complained that the doctor should have known, but apparently the medical records of the hospital are different from the ones in the emergency room, so the emergency-room doctors have no way of knowing what happens in the hospital or vice versa.

Every time we see Dr. Landers, he has to have Jan, his office assistant, call around to find out what was done at the emergency room or with this doctor or that. Sometimes he can't even figure out what he's prescribed before. Rebecca's chart is pretty big, and I guess it's pretty hard to find the information in all that paper. Besides, it's a wonder he can read what he's written! I can't figure out what the prescription says, his writing is so bad. The longer Rebecca has been sick, the more people we've seen. Everyone has an idea about how to help her get better, but I don't think they talk to each other, and each of them keeps his own records. I guess they expect us to make sure the information gets from one doctor to another, because they don't do it very well.

It sure would help if Dr. Landers could keep up to date with asthma treatment. Sometimes I feel like John and I know more than he does. We see the advertisements on TV and read everything we can get our hands on. We talk with anyone whose child has asthma. Landers is so busy that it's hard for him to stay up with all the changes. One visit, I remember, he pulled some samples out of his desk and offered them to us, saying, "This is a new asthma drug that's supposed to be good. Why don't you see if it will work? A drug salesman left them for me when he came by last week." The other thing we've noticed recently is that Dr. Landers gets impatient when we bring him our ideas and questions. I guess he doesn't have time for that, because he's always rushing from room to room to see patients.

John was really upset this morning when he called me. His partners told him he wasn't paying enough attention to the practice, so he didn't get the bonus he was hoping for. He told me he has to focus on this big case, and I have to cover Rebecca until the case is over. We argue about the bills. Last month we spent $900 on Rebecca's medications, office visits, and emergency-room visits. That's the worst it's been. Usually it's around $600, not counting special foods and bedding and other things we've had to do to make our home safer for Rebecca. Lucky my shop is doing okay, because otherwise we'd have to borrow to make it through until Rebecca outgrows this. As it is, we can't save very much.

Rebecca's illness is putting a lot of strain on John and me. When the other children have problems, it's overwhelming, and we fight. We never used to, at least not like we do now. The stress is getting to us. As if that wasn't enough, the counselor at Michael's middle school called to schedule a parent conference. I guess he's been acting up in class.

This is really a nightmare. We have to work so hard to get Rebecca taken care of that we don't have time for the rest of our family. John and I lose perspective and take it out on each other. I don't know how long we can keep this up.

# 2

# THE CHANGING FACE
# OF MEDICINE

THE CARE REBECCA receives fails her and her family. Not because Dr. Landers or the other specialists are poor physicians. They are rigorously trained and highly motivated. North City Hospital and its emergency room are well staffed and equipped, their physicians expert in handling medical emergencies. Rebecca has received the latest medicines, been treated in modern offices and emergency rooms, and been admitted to a state-of-the-art hospital. Her life has been saved on several occasions. These pieces of the medical-care puzzle are in place. But no matter how good the doctors and institutions are, they don't fit together very well and critical pieces are missing. Patients, especially those with chronic or complex illnesses, suffer as a result.

Strip away the professionals, the treatments, the equipment, and the institutions of modern medicine, and one finds that care is organized for an earlier, far different period of history. Medicine began as a craft practiced by independent, autonomous professionals who relied on one another only when they had to. Care was rudimentary, medical science in its infancy. Professionals helped people through illnesses and death with caring and compassion. They could offer little else. The same model persists to this day. It lies at the heart of our myths about the physicians and medical care we expect. The popular 1970s television program *Marcus Welby, M.D.* captured it well. Dr. Welby was a master of medical diagnosis and treatment, understanding with his patients, and fiercely independent. He was constantly on guard to save his patients from disease, unscrupulous physicians, and unfeeling administrators. Beneath his gruff exterior, as one would expect, was a heart of gold and a winning sense of humor.

But modern medicine is far removed from those simpler days. Marcus Welby is a dangerous fiction. Now at the beginning of the twenty-first century, medicine faces unprecedented challenges. Shifting expectations among those who require care, accelerating advances in medical science and technology, and the rapid growth in the number of people with chronic illnesses have changed the nature of medicine itself. Bewildering complexity, growing demand for transparency, expanding diversity within the U.S. population, and new threats to public health from international travel, migration, and terrorism have further stressed the craft-based autonomous physician model. Continuing to rely on this timeworn approach in the future carries unacceptable risks to patients and costs to our society. Medical care as organized today is obsolete. Fundamental changes in the relationship between patient and doctor and among professionals; a new design for the care of patients with complex illnesses; and the creation of organizations with the resources to support the integration and coordination of care for patients are required to complete the puzzle and enable patients to receive the best that medicine can offer.

## Seven Challenges Facing Medicine

### Challenge 1: The Changing Expectations of Patients

When I was in medical school in the 1960s, medical students were taught that patients, especially those with serious illnesses, became emotionally dependent on their physicians. This placed a special burden on the physician to honor that trust and protect the safety and privacy of each patient. The physician's role in this paternalistic model was to make the best possible medical decisions on the patient's behalf, helping the patient cope with their illness along the way. Patients were expected to accept this guidance unquestioningly and gratefully.

Today, patients expect their physicians to help them understand the choices, but they often want to make the decisions for themselves. Researchers recently asked women diagnosed with breast cancer if they wanted their physician to make the decision about their treatment, wanted to make that decision with the doctor, or wanted to make the decision themselves after talking with their physician, specialists, and other sources. Two-thirds of the women preferred partnership with the physician or independent decision-making; only one-third wanted the physician to decide for them.

Nearly 130 million Americans are connected to the Internet; health-related searches are one of the most common uses of the worldwide web. People over sixty-five years of age are a fast-growing user segment, and teenagers report that their web searches often involve health-related subjects. Books and magazines on health are popular. Patients often arrive for appointments carrying printouts and articles and expecting prescriptions for the drugs they've seen advertised. Baby boomers, used to making their own decisions and wary of authority, now care for their parents, provide for their children, and are fast approaching the age when many chronic illnesses appear. When this happens, as one colleague put it, "the medical-care system won't know what hit it!"

This growing independence is also reflected in the number of Americans seeking care outside the traditional medical system. Kaiser Permanente researchers found that between 18 and 25 percent of adult respondents in several U.S. cities regularly seek care from alternative sources. Medical consumers spend an estimated $40 billion annually on "nutraceuticals," dietary supplements and vitamins. A study of home-use disease-monitoring devices conducted by several medical device–manufacturing firms and medical organizations produced two conclusions. First, a growing market exists for such devices. Second, 70 percent of the test results generated at home never reached the medical record and were unavailable to the clinicians who work with those patients.

In spite of their growing independence, patients still expect to have a close, trusting, personal relationship with their primary physician. They also want to be partners with their doctors, drawing on the experience of their doctors to answer their questions, make informed choices, and manage their conditions. They want their care to be coordinated when they move from doctor to doctor and from institution to institution over the course of an illness. They want doctors to be consistent so that information moves seamlessly, medications are compatible, and care recommendations are not at odds with one another. Experiences in other parts of their lives shape their expectations for medical care. They can access their banks by ATM machine, via the Internet, or in person. They can receive technical support and advice around the clock, either online or from call centers, for the products they buy. Their mail can be tracked and delivered anywhere in the world, often within seventy-two hours. They can have ready-made dinners delivered to their home, buy precooked meals at the supermarket, eat food from around the world in fast-food outlets, dine in gourmet restaurants, or cook from scratch, depending on their mood and their finances.

These emerging expectations among patients have important implications for medical care. Physicians will be particularly affected. Doctors must be able to spend time with their patients to build the healing relationship at the core of good care. They must have the tools to provide information and the technologies that enable patients to communicate with them day or night. They must coordinate the care a patient receives outside their office. They must explore new ideas that patients bring them, yet follow the rules of evidence that govern sound medical practice. Their role must shift from all-knowing expert to collaborative partner. Doctors must do all this while seeing between twenty and fifty patients each day (depending on specialty) in visits that rarely last more than fifteen minutes and often occur in less than ten, and in relationships that involve a total of an hour or two a year together.

### Challenge 2: The Expanding Pace and Scope of Discovery in Medical Science and Technology

Responding to patients whose expectations are changing dramatically is hard enough, but physicians, medical professionals, and medical institutions also must keep up with advances in medical science and technology. Although the seeds of these advances are found in changes that began late in the nineteenth century, the most dramatic discoveries have occurred since 1950. Today we can identify, treat, and track the progress of diseases unknown fifty years ago with tools that have become more precise and easily used by patients each passing year.

The National Institutes of Health has existed for more than a century. But after World War II, it became a grant-making institution that supported scientific research in academic medical centers and dramatically expanded its influence in American medicine. For the last half of the twentieth century, its budget doubled every ten years (every twenty-two years in constant dollars); the budget doubled in 1997–2002 with large congressional appropriations. In 1990, the NIH had an annual budget of $8,505,256,000 and included twenty-four separate institutes. In 2001, the budget had risen to $20,548,928,000, and the number of institutes had grown to twenty-seven. The profitability of the pharmaceutical industry, its billions spent on direct-to-consumer advertising, and its $30 billion in funding for research in 2001 (a 16 percent increase over 2000) speaks to the impact these companies have on medical care and medical science. The biotechnology sector, focused on putting advances in genetics and protein chemistry to human and agricultural use, now includes some 5,000 companies worldwide since its launch in the late 1970s.

Rebecca, the asthmatic child described in chapter 1, is a beneficiary of these advances. In 1950, childhood asthma was believed to be caused by allergies, a high-strung, nervous personality, and family tensions. Medications were directed to relief of the tightness in the muscles that surround the small breathing tubes of the lungs. Few tools existed to monitor the illness, and none were available for home use. Today we know that asthma is caused by inflammation of the lining of the lungs and that it is best controlled by medicines that reduce or minimize these effects. The pharmaceutical industry has produced a host of drugs for children with asthma to complement powerful diagnostic and monitoring tools. Environmental triggers that provoke asthma attacks or irritate the lungs have been identified. We've learned that asthmatic children have significant improvements in health and quality of life when cared for by well-organized and supported teams of clinicians instead of by doctors who act independently.

New discoveries have occurred in most complex diseases that affect us. Within five to ten years, specific genetic information will be linked to early signs of disruption in specific proteins that presage the development of acute and chronic conditions. Breakthroughs in gene-array technologies will permit clinicians to make decisions about drugs and doses on the basis of individual receptivity. They will monitor our responses at the cellular level to adjust the dose and administration frequency, and they will be able to identify reactions and complications far earlier than is possible today.

Complementing these developments at the molecular level are advanced analytic techniques and powerful computers that help scientists examine large population groups to understand how social, environmental, and biological factors interact to affect our health. The National Nurses Health Study, initiated in 1976, examining the relationships between nutrition and chronic disease; the fifty-year Framingham Heart Study; and the studies supported by the MacArthur Foundation on factors that influence successful aging are three examples in a rich body of research. The same tools also enable us to compare approaches for organizing and delivering care.

Open a newspaper or listen to a news show and you are likely to learn about some promising medical advance. What is difficult to appreciate from the headlines is the relentless pace and remarkable scope of discovery. The growth in the number of randomized clinical trials published for medical professionals is telling. The randomized clinical trial, or RCT, is the gold standard for medical professionals, a rigorous study design that can provide important evidence about what works, for whom, under what circumstances. Leading medical journals impose strict requirements before articles are accepted for publication. "Juries" of clinician and scientist peers review each article to assure that the study has been executed properly and that results are important to medicine. In spite of these hurdles, an estimated 10,000 articles were published in 1999, and the average for the decade was nearly as high per year. During the 1970s, in contrast, it is believed that 500 RCTs were published annually.

This decade promises more of the same, as scientists predict that advances in the next ten years will dwarf those of the past fifty. Breakthroughs in molecular medicine, continued refinements in precision measurement tools, advances in telecommunications and computing technologies for medicine, and further exploration of the relationships among social, environmental, and biological factors in human disease are visible on the immediate horizon. What lies beyond is anyone's guess. The discoveries aren't limited to tools that help with medical diagnosis and treatment either. The Internet, personal computer technologies, and advances in telecommunications have changed how we connect with one another, get our questions answered, and carry out many of our daily tasks. Our nation's investment in science and technology is changing the world we live in; our expectations and how we interact with people and institutions are changing along with it.

The developments of the past fifty years and the likelihood of even more discoveries in the next decade place enormous demands on the medical-care system. They require more of physicians and medical professionals because almost always they increase the complexity of caring for patients: more physician specialists and other medical professionals; more support staff; more technology; more capital requirements; more care provided by more people. Six decades ago medical commentators expressed concern that doctors couldn't keep up. Today it's like trying to keep track of the daily commercial airline schedule in the United States, as one physician-leader described it. No individual, no matter how smart or how diligent, can do it without help.

The challenge goes well beyond keeping knowledge and skills current. Professionals must assess the value of these advances for their patients while scientists and statisticians argue over whether or not the evidence is compelling. They must bring the new science and technologies to the right patients, at the right time, and in the right way. Support staff must be trained, practices reorganized, and financing arranged to purchase the new technologies. Information must be collected from daily practice to refine the science and inventions through continuous improvement and learning. Care processes must be redesigned to coordinate among the professionals and prevent further fragmentation and confusion for patients. Patients require education to understand the differences between their beliefs and the emerging science and to accept the limitations and risks of the breakthroughs in spite of public hype or advertisements about their benefits. Professionals must figure out how they will be paid for these new practices. And they must do all this while meeting the needs of their patients every day.

## Challenge 3: The Increasing Number of Americans with Chronic Illnesses

At the start of the twentieth century, diphtheria, smallpox, and pneumonia and other infectious diseases, as well as trauma, were the major killers. People seldom lived long enough to develop cancer or Alzheimer's or other diseases of aging. One hundred years later, the situation has changed significantly. Today, chronic illnesses are the leading causes of death: heart disease, cancer, and stroke, often associated with smoking and obesity. Although infectious diseases still occur, of course, vaccines and effective antibiotics have eliminated many of the most deadly or made them amenable to treatment. Trauma, unfortunately, remains a leading cause of death among young men, although the causes today are automobile accidents and violence.

Nearly 50 percent of the U.S. population, approximately 125 million citizens, have at least one chronic condition (an illness that lasts more than three months); 44 million have at least two; and 37 percent of people over sixty-five years of age have three or more. Currently, 75 percent of direct medical expenses in the United States are devoted to chronic illness, approaching three-quarters of a trillion dollars annually. Hypertension affects 50 million people at a cost of $23 billion to $33 billion per year. Respiratory diseases affect 30 million people at a cost of $24 billion to $36 billion per year. Diabetes and cancer affect 16 million and 15 million individuals, respectively, and are remarkably expensive to treat. Estimates for cancer range from $37 billion to $107 billion; for diabetes, $44 billion to $98 billion. Heart failure, the leading cause of death in the country, affects 5 million people and costs $20 billion to $40 billion annually. Cancer ranks as the second leading cause of death, respiratory diseases the fifth, diabetes the sixth, and hypertension the tenth. Half the people with congestive heart failure, a condition in which the heart can no longer pump the blood effectively and fluids back up into the lungs and body, die within five years. There has been a 254 percent increase in hospitalizations for this condition in the past twenty years, resulting in 7 million hospital days.

Care for people with serious chronic conditions tends to be concentrated in the late stages of these illnesses. Aetna Insurance Company, one of the nation's largest medical-insurance companies, reports that care for late-stage, chronically ill patients involves just 16 percent of their total membership but requires 65 percent of the medical-care dollars Aetna spends each year. Patients with catastrophic, life-threatening complications of their illnesses are 1 percent of Aetna's insured population but consume 38 percent of the dollars available to pay for care.

The number of people with chronic diseases, and the resources required to care for them, will accelerate rapidly in the next twenty-five years. Today, 14 percent of the population is over sixty-five years of age. By 2030, demographers estimate that one in five Americans will be over sixty-five; many will be over eighty. The older we get, the more likely we are to develop chronic conditions, although chronic illnesses occur among children and working-age adults as well. By the year 2030, then, somewhere in the range of two of every three people in the United States will have at least one chronic condition, nearly half the population will have two or more, and 80 to 90 percent of medical expenditures will be directed to the care of people with these conditions.

Medical science has provided important tools for the diagnosis and treatment of chronic illness, just as for other conditions. When patients whose arteries feeding the muscles of the heart are blocked, for example, they can have new vessels moved from other parts of the body, artificial vessels inserted, or blockages shrunk through mechanical intervention and drug therapy. They can take medications and moderate their lifestyles with diet and exercise to reduce the chance of heart attacks. Surgery, chemotherapy, and radiation therapy can moderate the lethal effects of many cancers. The tool kit is expanding to identify and manage chronic conditions early in order to prevent more serious complications later. Understanding of how social, environmental, and biological factors interact to accelerate or decrease these illnesses and their complications continues to grow. And we are gathering important information about professional performance that can help patients make more informed decisions about their care. Within ten years, research in human genes and cells should enable us to know what chronic conditions we are at risk for well in advance of their appearance. This advance will trigger increased attention to what we do with that knowledge, leading to more education, prevention, and health-maintenance activities designed to minimize the risks we know we are facing.

The dramatic increase in the proportion of the U.S. population with chronic illnesses, and the sophisticated and expensive care required for these patients, have important implications for medical care. Chronic-disease care must be provided continuously, throughout a patient's life, rather than in interrupted visits when conditions flare up or acute complications arise. Care must be coordinated among the many professionals and institutions involved with such patients during the long course of these illnesses. Patients and their families become the primary caregivers where most care is provided—in the home and at work. Medical professionals with different backgrounds must work together to give the patient what he needs. Resources within the community must be called on to provide information and support. And professionals, especially physicians, must stay current with the changing diagnosis and medical treatment of these often complex and puzzling conditions.

## Challenge 4: The Growing Complexity of Medical Care

Medical care is mind-numbingly complex. Changing patient expectations, the expansion of medical science and technologies, and the increasing numbers of patients with chronic illnesses are part of the story. But it doesn't stop there. Medicine today involves a vast, fragmented, often isolated array of human, technical, and institutional resources. It operates in a labyrinthine legal and regulatory environment that makes Dante's *Inferno* look like a stroll in the park. And it conducts its business with systems so archaic and incentives so perverse that the nation's education system looks almost rational by comparison.

**Resources.**   Fully 17 percent of the nation's workforce is employed in medical care. The *categories* of medical professions have grown from ten in 1950 to more than 200 today, and there are over 100 recognized physician specialties today compared to a handful in 1950. Institutions we take for granted today were few and far between or didn't exist fifty years ago: nursing homes, hospice programs, visiting nurse organizations, ambulatory surgery centers, outpatient chemotherapy units, intensive care units, specialized operating rooms, new diagnostic imaging capabilities, and a host of new specialized procedure centers to do angiography and angioplasty, flexible sigmoidoscopy and colonoscopy, intraocular lens implants, and the many other procedures invented within the past half century. We have altered hospitals, changed the use of beds, and intensified staffing. Emergency rooms are often equipped with remarkable diagnostic and treatment technologies, and house specialty-trained physicians and nurses provide around-the-clock care. Highly specialized trauma centers serve patients who have suffered severe, often life-threatening accidents. Patients monitor their health in their homes, communicate with their physicians by email, and treat themselves following interactive video consultations. Medical dictation is done by doctors at hospitals, sent electronically to a medical transcription company in Southeast Asia, and returned to the doctors in twenty-four to forty-eight hours.

Medicine is also a huge business, consuming $1.4 trillion annually. Hospitals cost hundreds of millions of dollars to build, take years to plan, and require extensive permits and inspections before they can be opened. And then the real work begins. Equipment must be updated regularly, rooms maintained or remodeled as requirements change, and staffing shifted to match evolving diagnostic and treatment capabilities. A new CT scanner goes for $1.5 million and an MRI for $2.5 million. A state-of-the-art cardiac catheterization lab costs $1.8 million to equip. In round figures, the cost of building a new hospital is about $1.1 million to $1.4 million per bed depending on location; this means the cost of a 150-bed hospital is between $165 million and $210 million. Our nation's annual bill for prescription medications in 2001 was approximately $150 billion, up from $126 billion a year earlier. As in any sector in which huge dollars are at stake, the array of businesses, entrepreneurs, professionals, and hangers-on who want to feed at this monstrous trough grows larger and more varied by the day.

**Laws and Regulations.**   By the late 1990s, Mayo Clinic officials counted more than 130,000 pages of legal requirements and guidelines for Medicare, compared to 10,000 for the nation's Internal Revenue Service. Different parts of medical care are regulated under different laws and regulatory bodies that vary by state. Some twenty to twenty-five categories of medical professionals (doctors, nurses, pharmacists, etc.) report to their own state-licensing board operating under different laws in each state. Health insurance may be regulated by state insurance commissioners, by special agencies, or both, as in California. One area of law, called "body part legislation," prescribes what specific benefits must be covered by medical insurance, and sometimes specifies that care must be given a certain way by a specific professional or specialist. A blizzard of laws and new regulations is introduced in many states each session; similar levels of activity occur at the federal level. In 1999, for example, 906 health-related bills were introduced by the U.S. Congress, of which thirty-three were signed into law. The California state legislature introduced 512 pieces of health legislation in that year; 106 became law. These were not unusual years; this same pattern has occurred throughout most of the past decade.

The legal environment has grown more litigious as well. Plaintiff's attorneys have broadened causes of action for malpractice and awards have grown. Malpractice insurance premiums have risen dramatically. Class action suits brought against health insurers by plaintiff attorney syndicates and physician organizations have required millions of dollars to defend; to date, few have resulted in major settlements against the health-insurance industry. Tort reform has made little headway in spite of more than two decades of effort and growing concern on the part of practicing physicians and their professional organizations.

**Payment.**    Until the mid-1980s, the health-insurance and medical-payment system was relatively simple. The typical doctor or hospital filed claims with Blue Cross/Blue Shield and sent bills to patients for the balance, or they billed Medicare. Overhead was low and administration simple. Two developments changed this comfortable world: First, federal legislation made self-insurance attractive for employers; and second, the managed-care movement grew rapidly in the late 1980s. In spite of the many consolidations in the private health-insurance industry in the late 1990s, today's private doctor may work with as many as fifteen to twenty insurance companies and third-party administrators. A hospital may interact with even more. This is a significant administrative burden. It also makes the task of caregiving more difficult. Each insurer or self-insured plan has unique requirements regarding the professionals and institutions that can be used, the treatments provided, the benefits covered, and the patient's out-of-pocket financial responsibilities. The industry operates with no standard benefits package; no standard payment level or method; no standard cost-sharing formula between employer and employee; no standard billing practices; and no standard format for submitting claims. Disturbingly, this trend is accelerating in the rush to provide more options to payers and consumers in the name of consumer choice. The current trend to shift costs to the patient and to reduce benefit coverage will further aggravate the problem for physicians, especially those caring for patients with complex medical conditions. These illnesses are expensive and time-consuming to treat and require significant educational resources. Moreover, they extend over a long period of time, respond best to early intervention or prevention, and require constant vigilance to ensure that complications are identified and treated quickly. When financial and coverage considerations constrain clinical choices and create disincentives for patients to seek non-emergency care, the physician's job is made more complex than it already is. The patient suffers even more.

Payment for medical care is equally confusing. Fee-for-service payment, in which a doctor is paid for each specific thing he does, encourages doctors to do too much and rewards those who perform procedures and surgery instead of focusing on diagnosis, prevention, and education. Dr. William Richardson, chair of the Institute of Medicine studies on quality and safety, describes that system as "toxic to quality." Yet it remains the way most doctors and hospitals are paid. Attempts to pay providers a fixed amount of money for each person they are responsible for, so-called "capitation" payment, may encourage them to withhold care. Large delivery organizations like Kaiser Permanente, Group Health Cooperative (in Washington and Idaho), among others, have operated on a capitation model for decades with many safeguards and incentives to ensure that care is appropriate. Solo physicians and doctors in small group practices do not operate the same way and have had problems managing payments made in this form. Discounts, special contracts, bundling care payments for specific interventions (coronary bypass surgery, angioplasty, cancer care, etc.) to include doctor, hospital, pharmacy, and related costs can also be found scattered throughout the medical landscape.

The complexity of medicine places major burdens on its professionals and institutions. A physician may employ three to five support staff workers in his practice; the number has risen as business requirements continue to grow. The same trend is seen in medical institutions. Employees must be trained, managed, and developed to keep pace with changing medical practice. To avoid being swallowed completely by the fast-coalescing forces around them, professionals and institutions must employ sophisticated tools to manage daily practice, stay current with rapidly changing insurance requirements and payment arrangements, deal with the blizzard of regulations and legal threats, and handle communications among the caregivers. To increase bargaining power with insurers and share the costs associated with running their businesses, physicians must join together, hospitals must combine, and institutions must collaborate. Expenses have to be tracked closely to ensure that profits are sufficient to earn decent incomes with cash left over to invest in new technologies when they appear. As care involves hospitals, nursing homes, and special treatment facilities in addition to physicians' offices, systems must be able to capture what is done for each patient at each step regardless of location.

## Challenge 5: The Increasing Demand for Transparency

Only since late in the twentieth century have nonprofessionals been able to look inside the practice of medicine. Until then medicine was a black box, impenetrable to the lay public, zealously guarded by the medical professions. For decades, the public only knew whether or not hospitals had been accredited, whether or not physicians were licensed to practice, and whether or not physicians were board certified. In the 1980s, however, an important shift began. Driven by the emerging managed-care organizations and by purchasers who wish to understand what they are buying for their employees, the lid of the box has slowly been pried open.

Three major streams of activity changed the landscape. First, expanded institutional and health-plan accreditation processes have brought medical-care organizations and the doctors, medical professionals, and support resources who are part of them under close scrutiny. Second, quality and safety oversight and reporting systems added throughout the 1990s have brought greater accountability. Third, increasingly refined data on physicians and hospital performance has been placed in the hands of patients.

Today, the Joint Commission on Accreditation of Healthcare Organizations (JCAHO) and the National Committee for Quality Assurance (NCQA) carry out rigorous evaluations of hospitals, nursing homes, hospice programs, home health agencies, mental-health organizations, and managed-care organizations. Together with extensive performance data on compliance with prevention, care guidelines, and patient satisfaction, the information is made public through widely distributed reports. Moreover, Medicare, Medicaid, and many employers now require accreditation by either JCAHO or NCQA as a condition of offering: Failure to obtain accreditation means that business will be sent elsewhere. Several states add their own inspection processes to these independent accreditation efforts. In California, for example, under the aegis of the Knox-Keane legislation, inspectors join Joint Commission reviewers on accreditation visits.

Several federal-level activities are designed to provide greater insight into medical-system quality and safety performance. The National Quality Forum, an outgrowth of President Bill Clinton's Commission on Medical Quality in the United States, was constituted in 1999. This public-private partnership balances consumer, purchaser, payer, and provider interests in carrying out its mission to create quality and safety standards for use by accreditation organizations, purchasers of medical care, and state and federal oversight bodies. The National Practitioner Database, created by act of Congress in 1998, is designed to track malpractice and disciplinary actions against physicians and other clinicians caring for patients. Physicians, other medical professionals, hospitals, licensing boards, and regulatory agencies are required to submit information about legal or disciplinary actions taken against any medical professional. Access to the data is limited to licensing boards and regulatory agencies, but efforts by public groups and private citizens to open up the database continue. In 1996, Congress passed legislation calling for reporting standards, medical practice transparency, and medical-record security for patients throughout the country. The Health Information Patient Protection Act (HIPPA) could have significant implications for the medical-care system. Extensive reporting will be required, hastening the implementation of automated medical-information systems in doctors' offices that will make information on clinical practice more widely available.

Private purchasers, especially large employers, have led the development of "value purchasing" to improve medical service, quality, and affordability for their employees. Xerox Corporation was one of the earliest to undertake extensive evaluations of their medical offerings. Health plans and medical-care organizations were required to provide detailed information about performance of the plan, the professionals, and the institutions. This information was made available to employees during annual open enrollment periods; this and financial incentives were designed to encourage employees to choose higher quality, more affordable health-care coverage. Similar efforts are in place in a number of large corporations in the country. In addition, employer coalitions, such as the Pacific Business Group on Health, the Midwest Business Group on Health, and the Washington Business Group on Health, have experimented with how to use their extensive purchasing power to encourage medical-delivery systems to provide higher quality and more responsive care more affordably. CalPERS, the giant retirement-benefits manager for public employees in California, has recently announced plans to obtain more extensive data on system quality and safety and to use this information to drive improvements as part of its purchasing process. A very promising initiative is sponsored by the Leapfrog Group, made up of more than 100 large corporations and public insurers covering approximately 32 million medical consumers. Formed in 2000 in response to the Institute of Medicine's report on patient safety *To Err Is Human,* their goal is to improve patient safety by rewarding medical organizations and health plans that implement improvements known to enhance patient safety.

Finally, more information is being collected for direct distribution to patients and the general public. Typically, this effort has focused on surveys of patients to assess care and service. During President Ronald Reagan's term of office, the head of the Health Care Financing Administration (HCFA), Dr. William Roper, published for the first time extensive morbidity and mortality information on the nation's hospitals based on the Medicare experience. Today, numerous efforts are under way. The Foundation for Accountability (FACCT) prepares a variety of reports for consumers on medical-system performance. Advocacy groups like the National Partnership for Women and Family conduct extensive focus-group studies to determine what people want. The Kaiser Family Foundation, working with Professor Robert Blendon at the Harvard School of Pubic Health, has sponsored a comprehensive ongoing national study of consumer attitudes about medical care. Well publicized, the results can usually be found in leading newspapers and major policy journals. *Consumer Reports, U.S. News & World Report,* and *Newsweek* have published periodic rankings of managed-care plans and hospitals.

The black box of medicine is still slowly being forced open as public agencies and regulatory bodies, patient advocacy groups, public officials and lawmakers, and purchasers demand more transparency and accountability from medical professionals and institutions. And nothing on the horizon suggests that this trend will be reversed. The implications for medicine are clear. Professionals and institutions must be able to provide the data, understand the implications of the information, and act to improve their care using the findings. This capability requires increasingly sophisticated systems to capture and process the required data about their daily practices. They also must be responsive to the emerging information about patient preferences and assessments of the care patients have received. To respond, they must be able to educate their support staff and redesign office procedures and practices. Most of all, they must be prepared for the loss of independence and autonomy that they enjoyed for most of the last century. Public accountability is painful, especially when there has been so little for so long. But the forces demanding it are inexorable.

## Challenge 6: The Nation's Growing Diversity

Our nation is diverse, a rich mix of ethnic groups, religions, languages, and cultures. There is no longer a statistical ethnic or racial majority in California; more than 100 languages are spoken in the Los Angeles County School District. According to information from the Immigration and Naturalization Service (INS), the flow of immigrants seeking permanent residence in the United States grew from 600,000 per year in 1988–1990 to more than 900,000 per year by the turn of the century. Nonimmigrant temporary workers and foreign visitors approach 30 million per year, up from nearly 15 million in 1988. The INS estimates there are more than 5 million residents living illegally in the United States.

Wide disparities exist within our population in socioeconomic status, access to health insurance, ability to pay for medical services, and availability of medical services. Higher emergency-room use among people with lower incomes, more limited medical insurance, and lower educational levels mean that they wait longer to seek medical care, have more serious illnesses when they do, and require more significant and expensive medical interventions as a result.

Our diversity challenges medicine in several ways. Patterns of illness differ considerably according to ethnicity, culture, and socioeconomic status. Attitudes about health, illness, disease prevention, and treatment do, too. Each factor can influence how and when medical care is sought and how well medical recommendations are understood and followed. As effective as laboratory and imaging tools have become, the foundation for effective diagnosis and treatment still rests on a doctor's ability to understand what his patient is saying. Yet communications are difficult across the barriers of race, culture, language, and education.

Diversity places major demands on physicians, medical professionals, and medical institutions. A foundation for good care is the ability to recognize and treat the conditions specific to different groups as well as the illnesses that cross the boundaries of race, culture, and socioeconomic status. This standard isn't easy to attain now, even at current levels of understanding. As more sophisticated genetic information is linked to racial and environmental information, medical diagnosis and treatment will become even more challenging. Professional caregivers must also be able to communicate in the languages and cultures of their patients. If they cannot do it themselves, they must make sure they have people on their staff who can. Many women tend to be more comfortable with women physicians. Some patients relate better to professionals who share their social or racial backgrounds. Others are indifferent. Education and skill-development tools must be tailored to the needs and capabilities of the patients. Cultural competence affects medical care.

One anecdote from a national study to determine reading and comprehension levels among adults provides insight into how challenging this can be. A high-school educated mother brought her two-year-old daughter to the physician for treatment of an earache. The physician prescribed an antibiotic to be taken "orally four times a day." Several days later the mother was asked how she was giving the medicine. She responded that she didn't know what "orally" meant, so two times a day she gave the child the medicine by mouth and two times a day in the ears. She had also figured out how to fit the doses into the family's busy schedule. She gave all four doses in the morning before she left for work.

In addition to the knowledge and skills required, caregivers need data systems that can remind them about their patients' backgrounds and special concerns driven by their diversity. Physicians, medical professionals, and medical institutions must evaluate their cultural competence through ongoing interactions with their patients in order to improve their care and to ensure that their own assumptions are not off the mark. Data on race, culture, and socioeconomic status are essential for studies involving larger populations intended to identify disease patterns, develop appropriate interventions, and track results.

## Challenge 7: External Threats

As people travel more extensively around the world, and as more people come to the United States to visit or live, our nation's natural boundaries no longer protect us from infectious and environmental hazards in other parts of the globe. The most obvious example is the AIDS virus, believed to have been introduced into the United States by commercial airline personnel who had engaged in unprotected sex in Africa and then in New York City. There are others as well. Fortunately, no other infection has reached the epidemic proportions that AIDS has, in spite of well-publicized books and articles about the threats. But we remain vulnerable and must keep vigilant to avoid infectious disease that could devastate a vulnerable population. The threat does not stop there. The anthrax outbreak following on the heels of the September 11, 2001, terrorist attacks on the East Coast brought home the threat of bioterrorism.

A more remote public health threat with significant implications for the medical system is environmental. In their book *Thunder from the East,* authors Nicholas Kristol and Sheryl WuDunn assert that in the coming decades, environmental problems in rapidly industrializing China and other parts of Asia could affect the rest of the world. Significant health problems have already been reported in parts of China related to industrial pollution of air, water, and food. As with infectious diseases and terrorist threats, we must be on guard to ensure that health problems rooted in environmental causes are identified early should they occur, and that remedial actions are taken promptly when they do appear.

This challenge places major demands on the medical system. Information systems must be in place to track disease prevalence based on doctor office and hospital visits and to ensure speedy reporting to public health agencies. Disease recognition and treatment guidance must be distributed rapidly to doctors and other clinicians to help affected patients and avoid spread of the disease. Communications systems are required to enable professionals and public health officials to maintain contact during outbreaks and to give the public up-to-date information. Medical supplies must be tracked, production systems put in place, and distribution mechanisms carefully designed to ensure that critical materiel is available when needed. Public education is essential to prepare people for possible threats and to address their concerns when attacks actually occur. Emergency response capabilities must be highly developed and ready for mobilization. Coordination among medical, public, and law-enforcement officials is essential to safeguard the public and limit the damages.

## Is Medicine Ready for These Challenges?

Any one of these seven challenges places heavy demands on the medical-care system. Together, they are an avalanche that will continue to gain speed and momentum for the foreseeable future. Medicine as it is now organized is unprepared.

Today the majority of people who suffer from high blood pressure are unaware that they have the condition, and only one of four diagnosed with the disease receives care that works effectively. Most adults with diabetes don't know they are sick; of those who do, three of four are not monitored and medicated at a level sufficient to manage their blood sugar and the heart disease–causing fats in their blood, the primary causes of life-threatening complications for them. Atrial fibrillation, an irregular heartbeat often found in the elderly, can cause dangerous, even life-threatening blood clots, yet two of every three people diagnosed with the condition are not properly treated with blood thinner, the medicine that reduces the chance that clots will form in the first place. Three of four people who are depressed are untreated. Half of the people hospitalized with congestive heart failure will be rehospitalized within ninety days after they are discharged. Just one of two people over the age of sixty-five gets a flu shot. If you're a man with an enlarged prostate gland, your chances of being operated on will vary by 300 percent depending on where you live. Similarly, treatment for breast cancer, back pain, heart disease, and for almost every other medical condition varies depending on the community where one lives. Medical practices, it appears, are driven more by habit and local custom than by medical science.

It takes years for some proven treatments to reach patients, while others, especially procedures and new surgical techniques, are quickly incorporated into practice. As many as 80,000 people die of errors in hospitals each year. We do not know how many deaths from errors occur in nonhospital settings. But the number is likely to be higher because most care is given outside the hospital. Significant quality problems have been well documented in the medical literature. There is compelling evidence that the United States lags far behind other developed countries in critical indicators of good health even after correcting for the greater socioeconomic disparities and diversity in our country. In the 1996 Picker Institute study of American medical consumers, more than 70 percent in a national study sample described the medical system as a "nightmare to navigate, . . . impersonal, confusing, demeaning, unresponsive." In a Harris poll conducted in 2000, 65 percent of people between the ages of fifty and sixty-five suffering from at least one chronic illness indicated that their care was less than satisfactory; 50 percent of those over sixty-five agreed.

And of course, medical care is frightfully expensive, consuming 13.9 percent of the gross national product, and with no end in sight. After a period of low price increases during the middle years of the 1990s, health-insurance premiums are now escalating at double-digit rates, just as they did in the early 1990s. Pharmaceutical prices have increased 12 to 20 percent per year for the past several years. New technologies add further costs; hospital and physician charges have climbed dramatically; and more costs are being shifted to individual consumers as employers seek new ways to deal with the escalating cost spiral. Finally, we know that significant disparities in health status exist from one socioeconomic class to another; from one racial group to another; between genders; and among people of different ages.

Our nation's response to the anthrax outbreak in late 2001 and early 2002 provides a window into the problems our medical-care system has in dealing with external threats. Recognition of the illness was delayed because few physicians and emergency-room personnel had ever seen the disease. It was unclear whether or not exposed individuals should receive preventive treatment in the absence of symptoms. Treatment recommendations were confusing. Communications to practicing physicians were haphazard. No authority could speak on behalf of the medical establishment to a frightened and confused public. Vaccinations and antibiotics were not available for those who needed them. And this was a relatively minor outbreak; less than ten people died.

In three recent studies of medical care in the United States, the expert panels constituted by the Institute of Medicine of the National Academy of Sciences reached the following conclusions:

Serious and widespread quality problems exist throughout American medicine. These problems ... occur in small and large communities alike, in all parts of the country, and with approximately equal frequency in managed care and fee-for-service systems of care. Very large numbers of Americans are harmed as a result (*Quality of Care in America*, 1998).

Errors are responsible for an immense burden of patient injury, suffering and death (*To Err Is Human*, 1999).

A serious and persistent disconnect exists between the promise of medical care delivery and what happens in reality. This is not a gap, but a chasm (*Crossing the Quality Chasm*, 2001).

In spite of all that we invest in medical care and medical science, the care we receive is failing us. It has not responded to the seven challenges it faces, nor can it do so as long as it remains organized as it is now. The seductive model of the autonomous, independent physician-craftsman is as ill-suited to meet the demands of modern medicine in a complex modern society as the Pony Express would be to deliver our mail, the telegraph would be to communicate with one another, or the horse and buggy would be to transport us from one city to the next.

# 3

# ADAM LANDERS, M.D.:
# THE SOLO PRACTITIONER

*Dr. Adam Landers, the solo general pediatrician described below, is fictional. But his story is typical of that of many doctors in small or solo practices and represents the day-to-day routines and challenges they face in today's medical environment.*

DR. ADAM LANDERS has practiced alone for fifteen years. Almost everyone he knows—medical-school classmates and residents with whom he trained in pediatrics—practices this way or joined small, single-specialty groups of less than ten physicians. Only a few have chosen to work in larger groups. There was no exposure to these arrangements during medical training, and faculty physicians believed that larger medical groups could compromise a doctor's professional independence.

## Long Hours and Hard Work

Dr. Landers is a hard worker. He sees about thirty patients each day in the office, five days a week, schedules evening office hours one night a week, and has Saturday morning office hours twice each month. Routine well-baby and well-child visits are scheduled on Tuesday and Thursday afternoons to separate healthy and sick children. He alternates night and weekend emergency calls each week with another community pediatrician, and he follows his own patients when they need to be hospitalized at North City Hospital. His day starts at 7 A.M. when he begins rounds. If he doesn't have patients in the hospital, he arrives at his office by 8 A.M. and uses the time to catch up on paperwork: insurance forms, medical records, and correspondence. He schedules patients from 8:30 A.M. until noon and again from 1 P.M. until 5:30 P.M. He spends between five and ten minutes with each patient; the rest of the time the patient is getting in and out of the waiting room, undressing for the exam, having lab and X-ray studies done, or waiting. He'll spend a little more time, fifteen to twenty minutes, with patients with difficult problems or families new to his practice. Usually he leaves for home by 6:30 P.M. after he finishes more paperwork and the last of the twenty phone calls he makes each day. He gets three or four more phone calls from parents each evening because he encourages them to call "day or night" with their questions. Most evenings, he attends meetings at the hospital or his local medical society or tries to catch up with several medical journals. Once a month he meets with his six support staff members for lunch to talk about the practice, discuss problems, and consider possible changes to the practice routine. Except for that meeting, he uses the noon hour to complete his morning patient records and make phone calls. He also sees drug and medical-supply salesmen, who bring him up-to-date information about their products and provide free samples for him to distribute to his patients and staff.

## Seeing Patients

Dr. Landers and his staff have a well-organized routine to see patients. After patients check in with the receptionist, Anne Patterson, they wait in the reception area until his office assistant,

Maria Hernandez, calls them back to the exam room. Maria finds out why they've come in that day, weighs them, takes their temperatures, checks their immunization status, and records the information on the office medical record. Dr. Landers expects specific laboratory tests for each type of patient. Healthy children in for a routine checkup have one set of tests, a child with a sore throat receives another, and Rebecca and other children with asthma undergo still others. By the time Dr. Landers sees the patient, he has already reviewed the patient's medical record, including the lab results, and the information recorded by Maria or her colleague, Jan Arlington, who works on Maria's days off and does the lab and X-ray studies. He greets the parents if they're in the exam room (when a child gets to be ten or eleven, he likes to see them separately, although this isn't a hard-and-fast rule), then turns his full attention to the child. Asking questions while he examines the patient, a process that requires no more than two to three minutes, he can usually figure out what's wrong right away. The rest of the time, Dr. Landers writes in the chart and explains to the patient and parents what he plans to do. He writes out the prescriptions and may order additional laboratory and X-ray exams, depending on the diagnosis. Sometimes, when he thinks it's necessary or when parents ask, he will refer a patient to a specialist. As a general pediatrician, though, he takes care of most problems himself. At the end of every visit, he asks the parents and the child if they have any questions. Then he's on to the next exam room. He wastes little time with small talk during the day and rarely gets behind in his schedule. Only when children have urgent medical problems does he alter his routine; somehow he usually manages to squeeze them in. He's rarely called to the emergency room at North City during his office hours, because the ER staff knows that he likes to have them handle the problem if they can. When he does have to cancel scheduled patients to take care of a sick child in the emergency room or hospital, his office staff has to rearrange appointments for all the affected patients; never an easy or pleasant task. He also has to see more patients in shorter visits for several days before he can get back on a normal schedule.

## Medical Records

Dr. Landers has devised a medical-records system to keep track of each patient. In medical school and during his residency, he was taught to record patient information in a problem-oriented and SOAP format: subjective historical information; objective findings from the physical examination and from lab and X-ray studies; analysis of the problems; and plans. A problem list and medication list was also required at the front of each medical record. In his busy practice, this approach proved too time consuming and cumbersome, so he has developed shorthand for recording important information. He writes brief notes in the patient's record when he finishes each visit to jog his memory the next time he sees the patient. He has always tried to keep comprehensive records for his more difficult patients when time permits.

## Referrals

Dr. Landers is careful about referring his patients to other doctors. He doesn't want to lose them from his practice, and he wants to make sure he trusts the specialists he uses. Several are former medical-school classmates or physicians whom he met during his residency; most he sees at the hospital or various social events. When a patient is referred, such as when Rebecca was referred to the allergist, Dr. Landers usually faxes information from the medical chart. Occasionally, he dictates a letter summarizing the condition, the studies, and the treatments, especially when the patient has a complex medical history or is being sent to a major medical center. He and his colleagues understand how each likes to work, and there's always the phone if the matter is more serious. Each clinician decides how he wants to care for his patients, keeps his own medical records based on what works best for him, and makes independent decisions about other referrals, hospitalization, or treatment plans. Occasionally a specialist calls Dr. Landers to provide an opinion about what should be done for a patient. Dr. Landers and his colleagues rarely explore options together to arrive at a shared plan of action for a particular patient; they refer patients to one another, but they work separately. Rarely one of them will refer a patient to a nonphysician medical professional in the community, a nurse practitioner or child psychologist. Generally, though, they prefer to have their patients taken care of by another physician.

## Lab and X Rays

Dr. Landers can do routine laboratory tests and X rays in his office. For more demanding lab exams, patients are sent to a large, commercial lab in the community that Landers likes, or to the hospital laboratory. Landers has confidence in the four-man radiology group in town that he uses for more sophisticated exams, and he sometimes asks them to read X rays taken in his office when he is unsure of the results. More demanding studies are done at North City Hospital, and there's always the University Medical Center for unusual, highly sophisticated studies.

## Support Staff

In addition to his full-time medical assistants, Maria and Jan, and the receptionist, Anne, Dr. Landers employs three part-time support staff people to deal with the growing administrative load in his office. Anne checks people in for their doctor visits, confirms insurance coverage, records the services Dr. Landers provides to each patient, makes follow-up appointments, provides referral physician numbers to those needing them, screens the forty to sixty incoming phone calls received throughout the day, and collects copayments and fees from patients at the end of a visit. She also sorts mail, paying close attention to laboratory and X-ray results so that Dr. Landers sees them as soon as they arrive.

Two half-time clerks manage the billing process for the practice. Dr. Landers sends bills to seventeen different insurance companies, including the seven with whom he has contracts for discounted fee-for-service care. Each requires a different form and has its own rules. Dr. Landers has to go over the forms each day to check for mistakes before he signs them. Although the clerks have been with him for several years, they still make errors that cause the insurance company to delay payments or refuse to pay altogether. The other part-time clerk helps Anne and the medical assistants with referrals. Dr. Landers only makes two or three referrals a day. The clerk can put together the necessary medical information based on directions from Dr. Landers, or from Maria and Jan, and ensure that it gets to the right doctor. She also follows up with patients to see if they've been able to arrange things with the specialist and to remind them to return to Dr. Landers for follow-up. The referral clerk also helps Dr. Landers and Anne with office correspondence.

## The Business of Solo Practice

The business side of Dr. Landers's practice demands considerable time and attention, sometimes as much as twenty hours a week on top of the nearly forty hours a week he spends in his office seeing patients. He collects about 90 percent of what he bills; he can't collect the rest, either because he can't get people to pay, even after they've been dunned by the collection agency he works with, or because the insurance companies reject his claims. Even when claims are accepted, the companies are often slow to pay. Meanwhile, he has to pay his staff, his office rent, and his malpractice and equipment insurance; purchase supplies and equipment; and pay monthly fees for his automated practice-management system. His overhead expenses are about the same as those of the other pediatricians in his community, but somewhat lower than what other specialists have to spend. One surgeon colleague he knows has three times the overhead he does because of the specialized equipment, high malpractice premiums, and large staff required for his particular practice.

Because Dr. Landers is paid a fee for each patient he sees and for every service he provides, he has to produce a certain number of visits every day to "make his nut," as he puts it. He often reminds his wife that the morning patients pay to keep the office open; the afternoon patients pay him. He can't take too long with any one patient, as he can't bill enough to cover his time when he does. He once considered hiring a registered nurse to fill a vacant medical-assistant position, but he chose Jan instead because she was less expensive and could do the lab and X-ray work, too. At one point, three years ago, he looked into bringing a pediatric nurse practitioner into the practice. The costs were high, and he didn't think he could bill enough to cover them without reducing his own income. Besides, he didn't like the idea of working that closely with another clinician.

If he is ill or gone from the practice, he loses money. Revenues drop nearly to zero even if his staff keeps the office open to take phone calls, see a few patients for follow-up lab and X-ray work, and complete administrative chores. He's diligent about scheduling one week each year to attend a pediatrics refresher course, though he has to close his office to do so. The courses are usually held in nice resorts, so he combines his ongoing education and personal time off with his wife. He takes one week of vacation with his family each summer and another during the Christmas holidays.

## Buying Equipment and Malpractice Insurance

Dr. Landers must make sure his office and medical equipment is up to date and working properly. He has to plan carefully for each investment because he has little capital for major purchases, except for a small line of credit at his bank. Financing is a headache. His accountant, Jim Horner, meets with him every two weeks to help with financial planning and tax matters and to advise him on office and personal investments. Dr. Landers buys malpractice insurance through his local medical society. He has only recently incorporated an automated practice-management system into his practice to help with billing and administrative matters; the crossover to the new system has taken longer than he expected, so he hasn't yet seen any financial benefits from the investment. He doesn't have the time or interest to automate the clinical side of his work—medical records, lab and X-ray results, prescriptions—and couldn't anyway because the costs and loss of revenues while he learned the system would be prohibitive.

## Keeping Up

Dr. Landers prides himself on being a good doctor. He graduated from an outstanding medical school, was trained in one of the best pediatrics residency programs in the country, and successfully obtained his certification from the American Board of Pediatrics. He attends the annual refresher course in general pediatrics, subscribes to four pediatrics journals, and belongs to a journal club of community pediatricians that meets monthly to review interesting articles. He has passed the written exams to maintain his specialty certification. State licensure requirements for continuing medical-education hours have posed no problems either.

But he feels as though he's falling further and further behind, and it seems as though he has to work harder to keep up each year he's in practice. He doesn't like to rely on drug salesmen for information on new drugs; he knows that no matter how honest they are, their information is biased in favor of the products they represent. Except for the medical meetings, he doesn't get a chance to talk with his colleagues about new ways to care for patients or how to deal with difficult cases. More and more often, his patients bring fistfuls of printouts from the Internet, copies of articles, and chapters from books to discuss with him during their children's visits. They often know more than he does about new treatments. He can't afford to take the time to go through these materials with them or to do independent research when he can't answer their questions, though. And the online medical information Internet links he has tried are too slow, so he's pretty much given up trying to keep up that way. He has received written diagnostic and treatment guidelines from the American Academy of Pediatrics, his national specialty organization, but he doesn't usually get to them during the day. He tries to review them when he has time at night and makes sure they're updated when new ones are developed.

He was embarrassed recently when he finally referred one of his patients to a pediatric endocrinologist. The mom had been badgering him for months with ideas she'd gotten off the Internet about why her seven-year-old child was so small and got tired so easily. She kept insisting that it had something to do with growth-hormone deficiency. He didn't think it did. The pediatric endocrinologist, it turned out, has nearly forty patients with the problem; she recognized it immediately, started growth-hormone therapy, and the child is already responding.

## Happy to Practice Alone

In spite of the pressures of solo practice, Landers is happy practicing alone. He organizes his practice and takes care of patients the way he chooses; if he wants to try something new, he can. When he decides to change something, he tells his office staff. He doesn't have to make the day-to-day compromises in the way he cares for patients or runs the office that he would if he had a partner. He likes his patients and most of the parents he deals with and relates well to them. Word of mouth from one parent to another, in fact, is his main source of new patients. He enjoys being part of the medical community, where he is respected as a pediatrician and involved with his colleagues in hospital and medical-society issues. He has a full social life and a rewarding family life with his wife and two teenage children. Although he'd like to spend more time with them, especially now, he feels he has reached a workable balance between the demands of his profession and the needs of his family.

## Insurance Companies

The only thing Dr. Landers would like to change is the incessant demand from the insurance companies for more information and more justification every time he sends them a bill. He has had to add one and a half people to his staff to handle what required only a part-time person when he first started in practice. In the early 1990s, he joined his colleagues in fighting the managed-care companies that were trying to control his medical-care decisions, interfere with his referral relationships, and reduce his fees. He lost money on several capitation contracts with three managed-care companies in which he was paid a fixed amount for each patient in his practice, regardless of whether or not he provided any care. Fortunately, most of the companies retreated from their more intrusive approaches in the late 1990s. Now they are just picky about fees and allowable claims.

And of course, they're trying to shift more costs onto the family by reducing benefits and increasing copayment requirements. This arrangement might be good for the insurance companies and the employers, but it causes all sorts of problems for his patients and his practice. His patients often need more care than they are covered for, so the family has to pay the difference. This expense, together with the increased copayments for office visits, lab tests, X rays, and everything else, it seems, means that he has to hire more staff to collect payments. He has had to raise his fees to cover these costs, so it seems like no one's better off.

Dr. Landers can't afford to spend the time with parents and children who want to have their questions answered or explore their choices with him. He doesn't have many educational tools to help them, either: the videos, the educator-run groups, the written materials. Advances in medical science and technology are overwhelming him. Because of time pressures during the day, he must rely on his memory, then tries to go to his written sources at night. The demands of practice make it difficult for him to reorganize his routines or train his staff when he changes his approach.

Landers's practice isn't designed to care for a patient with a chronic illness. He and his support staff can't take the time and don't have the tools to train the patient or the family to function as primary caregivers. His medical-records system is cumbersome, and information is hard to access. He has no system to remind him of things he must do when a patient comes in for a follow-up visit. He can't easily access his medical records to see how well patients with a particular diagnosis are doing with the care he has provided them. When more physicians become involved, the care fragments further. By the time a patient has been cared for by several physicians and a large number of medical professionals in doctors' offices, emergency rooms, hospitals, and nursing homes, the process has become a chaotic maze. Critical information is hidden in each record. Treatment decisions are made at each stop without the benefit of shared approaches or common information. The patient and family must put it all together because they're the only ones who are in touch with what's happening every step of the way.

Whether finding office space, hiring and managing support staff, choosing and financing office equipment, collecting revenue and paying bills, negotiating with insurance companies, arranging malpractice insurance and dealing with malpractice actions, or keeping track of the benefit and payment options for each patient, Dr. Landers is on his own. He has no way to reduce costs by joining with other physicians to carry out "back-office" administrative functions. He can't afford to hire experts to help him with key management decisions. He is no match for the expertise or muscle that insurance companies have. The malpractice insurance company he works with is spread so thinly across the doctors of the state that he gets only modest help in identifying changes in practice procedures that could reduce his malpractice risks.

Fortunately, Landers flies below the radar when it comes to the national trends for more transparency and accountability. Most of those efforts have not yet reached him. Nonetheless, several of the insurance companies demand access to his records and want performance and compliance data, which he must produce by hand, working with his office staff. The companies need the information to meet NCQA accreditation requirements. This means a lot of overtime for his staff and extra nights and weekends for him because none of the clinical information is automated.

Patients who speak English and were raised in white, middle-class environments do well in Landers's practice. Maria serves as a translator for Spanish-speaking families. But as his practice grows more diverse, he has more difficulty meeting the needs of patients from different ethnic groups. He has a hard enough time keeping up with general pediatric medicine.

Dr. Landers is also out of the loop when it comes to new infectious-disease threats that occur because of international travel or bioterrorism. What he does learn comes from the media, although he tries to review the weekly newsletter from the Centers for Disease Control and Prevention (CDC) to keep up. Often some outbreak that occurred during the previous year is reviewed during the annual refresher course he attends long after the incident. He is diligent about complying with reportable disease requirements for the state and CDC, but this system is not automated. As a result, findings are not summarized and returned to him and his colleagues until several weeks have gone by. He relies on a former classmate who is on the medical-school faculty to find out about treatment recommendations for unusual infectious conditions, rather than waiting for the CDC or the state health department. When it comes to the exotic diseases, he is in the same boat as everyone else.

In spite of his motivation to be a high-quality physician, Dr. Landers can't deliver on the promise of modern medical care. He lacks the time, the money, and the organization to do so. And he will fall further and further behind if he continues to practice as he does today. Unfortunately, his patients and their families are the ones who pay the price. For the simple and routine illnesses, he provides a valuable service. But for more complex illnesses and chronic conditions, neither he nor his colleagues in other solo and small group practices are prepared for what medicine now requires and patients demand. The forces are too strong and the changes too profound. Physicians like Dr. Landers and his colleagues—independent, autonomous professionals who practice as craftsmen, alone or in small, single-specialty groups—are already being overwhelmed by those forces; as a consequence, the dangerous and expensive gulf between what patients need and expect and what they get grows wider every day.

# 4

# REBECCA, AGES SIX TO NINE: ASTHMA CARE WITH A TEAM

*The following account, from the perspective of Rebecca's mother, shows some of the benefits of a coordinated team-based approach to medical care as it affects the life of Rebecca and her family.*

I REMEMBER WHEN John gave me the bad news. His firm had changed health-insurance coverage. The new plan that let us continue with Dr. Landers was too expensive. We couldn't afford it. Then he told me the alternative, and I couldn't help crying. It was a plan with its own doctors and hospitals, so we'd have to find a new doctor for Rebecca and the other children, a new emergency room, move our records. Who knows who we'd see when we got there? Long waits. Never get the same doctor. Foreign doctors. I'd heard the horror stories from my friends, and I'd seen the movie *As Good As It Gets*. Going with the more expensive plan wasn't an option though.

So the next day I got busy. The first thing I did was call everybody I knew who belonged to this plan. Boy, did I grill them! Who are the good doctors? How do I get an appointment?

Which medical offices should I go to? By the end of the day, I had a list of several pediatricians, two internists for John, and a gynecologist that Missy Carlson, who owns the shop next to ours, goes to and likes. At least I had some ideas about who to ask for. But it took forever to get the phone answered that I was supposed to call for appointments. Finally someone answered who helped me arrange appointments for three kids on the same morning, for me with the gynecologist Missy had recommended, and for John with one of the internists.

The people at Dr. Landers's office were pretty upset when I asked them to send the kids' records to the new plan. Anne, the receptionist, told me it would be an assembly line and the doctors weren't any good. When I hung up I started to cry again, and it took me over an hour to calm down. By the time the kids got home, I had a splitting headache.

The clinic was large and filled with people when we got there for the children's appointments. It seemed pretty disorganized with everyone coming and going. But at least it was clean and the staff was reasonably friendly. Mildred Sernick and her daughter, Samantha, a friend of Rebecca's, stopped on their way out when they saw us. They said they liked the pediatrician we'd chosen. The visits didn't take long for Michael and Jen. The pediatrician, a tall, thin young woman, didn't seem old enough to be a doctor. She was very serious and asked questions quickly before she asked us to leave so she could examine Jenny alone, then Michael.

Michael and Jen went back to the waiting room, and Dr. Wilkensen asked about Rebecca. We talked for nearly thirty minutes and she covered everything: medicines, hospital visits, emergency visits, what we were doing for her now, how she was doing in school, even how we were coping with Rebecca's illness. Then she asked if it would be all right to talk with Rebecca alone and examine her at the same time. I didn't have any problems with that. Rebecca looked nervous, but I could see her sit up straighter, watching the doctor with a quizzical look on her face.

When the doctor called me back into the room with Rebecca, she said, "Rebecca and I have had a good talk. You've got a very brave girl here, you know."

Rebecca smiled and blushed, but she was calmer than I'd seen her with adults before. The doctor continued.

"Rebecca's got pretty severe asthma, so I'd like to bring in our asthma team to help us take care of her."

"But who'd be Rebecca's doctor?" I asked. I sure didn't want to make another change.

"I'll work with Dr. Foxton, who leads the program. You'll see him and continue to see me, too. Dr. Foxton works with a great team of people who are experts in asthma care. We work together. I'll help Rebecca for her general needs, and Dr. Foxton, the team, and I will take care of Rebecca's asthma."

Rebecca piped up then.

"Mom" (not "Mommy," which she'd called me forever). "Mom. Dr. Wilkensen has told me about Dr. Foxton and the asthma team. I want to try it."

"You seem to have me outnumbered," I joked. "Let's go ahead."

Dr. Wilkensen smiled briefly, then called in her nurse and asked her to walk us over to the Asthma Clinic to see Dr. Foxton.

Dr. Foxton was a short, intense, older physician. He seemed friendly enough, and, after greeting me, he squatted down to talk with Rebecca.

"Got some trouble with your lungs, huh?" he asked her. She nodded gravely.

"I've got *asama* and Dr. Wilkensen told us you'd help her take care of us." Rebecca's voice was steady as she returned his gaze.

"Do you think you can make it until Thursday?" he asked Rebecca.

"Yes. I think so," she replied.

Dr. Foxton asked me if I would be okay waiting until then.

"I can work you in today if we really need to," he suggested. "But if we can wait until Thursday, I can order laboratory work, review your records, check X rays, and spend more time with you. It's up to you, though."

"I think we can wait, Mom," Rebecca said quietly.

"Who is this child?" I wondered to myself, while agreeing to set up an appointment three days later. Dr. Foxton asked one of the nurses to get us the "starter packet" to take home and to arrange the usual laboratory and X-ray workup. "Your home-work," he called it. Then, "See you Thursday. Here's my card with my phone numbers and email address. You should already have Dr. Wilkensen's card. Call us if anything happens between now and then, or if you have questions that can't wait. One of us will be here. And by the way, we like our new families to spend the whole morning with us. We have a lot to go over in that first visit."

One hour later, Rebecca, Michael, Jen, and I were on our way. We had stopped by the laboratory in the clinic. The X-ray exam was quick, too, and then we were done. Rebecca walked in front of her sister and brother as I hurried to catch up. All the way home, Rebecca chatted on and on about Dr. Wilkensen and Dr. Foxton, her appointment Thursday, and the blood tests. Finally, the others told her to cool it. They weren't used to seeing her so animated.

That night, John and I went through the materials in the starter packet. The parents' questionnaire took us nearly half an hour to complete. There were lots of questions about our family, what we felt comfortable with doing to take care of her, and what we'd already done around the house to help her. The written pamphlets were pretty similar to what Dr. Landers had told us and agreed with other things I'd read about asthma. There was also a description of how the asthma team worked. That idea again. I wanted Rebecca to have one good doctor, not a committee. It was as simple as that. By the time we finished, John and I were pretty worried. This didn't seem like the right thing to do; there were too many people involved. Was Dr. Wilkensen or Dr. Foxton going to be there when we needed them? The next day, Rebecca read her packet after school and spent most of dinner telling her brother and sister about how the lungs work, what asthma is, and how she is going to take care of herself. I didn't realize she knew that much about her illness, and I'd never seen her interested in taking care of herself before.

Our visit Thursday started with Dr. Foxton, who spent nearly an hour asking Rebecca and me questions, going over the information that Dr. Wilkensen had written in the medical record that she and Dr. Foxton shared, showing us the laboratory and X-ray work, and examining Rebecca (with me in the room). For the last few minutes, Dr. Foxton explained what he wanted to do.

"Rebecca has a pretty serious asthma problem," he began. "She's already tried several of the drugs we use. But I'd like to put her back on two of them, add a couple of others, and see how she does."

He explained that he wanted Rebecca to take a five-day course of prednisone to reduce the inflammation in her lungs, supplemented by another medicine in an inhaler, four to six puffs every three to six hours to relax the muscles in her breathing tubes. Another drug in an inhaler was to be used for a week only, with three puffs twice a day, also to help get a handle on the chronic inflammation in Rebecca's lungs. He also prescribed one tablet a day to help keep inflammation from getting out of hand again.

Then he asked Rebecca if she was ready to learn how to use a peak flow meter to help her keep track of how well her lungs were working. She nodded seriously. Dr. Foxton demonstrated its use and asked Rebecca to try it. After a few false starts, she started to get the hang of it.

"Now," Dr. Foxton said to both of us, "here's what I want you to do." After making several entries on his computer, he printed out a written plan for how Rebecca should test herself and change her medicines—the doses and the frequency—depending on what her peak flow meter's results were. To keep things simple, peak flow results were divided into green, yellow, and red zones, each signaling a different level of control and requiring a different response. In the written plan were instructions for what we needed to do in each case.

Before leaving the exam room, Dr. Foxton asked us to spend time with Louise Morrison, the nurse who works on the asthma team. Louise took us to her "office," a crowded room filled with books and pamphlets. First she asked if we'd had a chance to read the starter packet information, and if so, if we had questions. Rebecca jumped in first.

"What's a *bronch-i-hole*?" she asked.

Using the life-sized model of the lung on her desk, Louise showed Rebecca the bronchiole. It's a small breathing tube that connects the air sacs of the lung with the big tubes that carry fresh air into and used-up air out of the lungs. She also described how the bronchioles get sore and irritated, and then swell and stiffen to cause asthma attacks.

We went over the written instructions again. Louise carefully explained how much Rebecca should take of each medicine, when she should take it, how she could change the dose depending on how she was feeling, and what the peak flow meter readings meant. She helped Rebecca use the peak flow meter, showing me what to look for, how to read the results, and how to make sure Rebecca used the meter properly. She reemphasized what Dr. Foxton had told us about modifying the medications based on the peak flow meter results. Before we left, she said to Rebecca, "Let's check one more time, Rebecca. Show me how you plan to use the meter."

Louise made one or two minor adjustments, then congratulated Rebecca on how quickly she'd learned how to manage things. As we left, Louise indicated that we should talk with the pharmacist if we had any questions when we picked up the medicines. She also gave us an 800 number to call "anytime, day or night, any day of the year" if we were worried about Rebecca or had questions. She explained that the call center was staffed by RNs familiar with asthma and the treatment protocols used in the asthma program. She also gave us the website address for the plan's online advice system. Finally, she indicated that one of her colleagues on the team, Ercilia Javier, a visiting nurse, would come to our home to help us organize things better for Rebecca and answer any questions we might have at that time. And she gave us a list of times when groups of parents with children with asthma get together to share ideas and concerns, working with her and Dr. Foxton. At the same time, she explained, another team member meets with the children and answers their questions, too.

That night I went through the written information describing the new treatments, showed John how to help Rebecca use the peak flow meter, and tried to summarize all that Rebecca and I had heard that morning. By the end of the evening we felt more informed than we had before, but we were still skeptical about whether this "team" idea would work for Rebecca.

A week later, Ercilia Javier came to see us. John had arranged to get away from the office for an hour, so he joined Rebecca and me in walking through the house with her. Ercilia pointed out bedclothes and pillows that could contain the mites known to "trigger" asthma attacks. She also showed us how to clean and dust to remove most of the dust molds known to bring on asthma attacks. When I asked about pets, she explained that although it's better not to have them, there are ways to brush them and clean the house to reduce the chances of asthma reactions. For the last half hour of her visit, she went over the medicines, asked how we were giving them, suggested some minor corrections, and made sure Rebecca was using the peak flow meter properly and that John and I were reading it correctly. As she left, she reminded us of the call number and the online system, gave us her card, and invited us to contact her or any of the team members if we had questions.

Three weeks later, when Rebecca woke up in the middle of the night crying and grunting and wheezing, my heart sank. We'd been so careful about her medications and had tracked her peak flow meter results compulsively. We'd been to the clinic for another long session with the health educator, had met briefly with Dr. Foxton, and had purchased new bedclothes and pillows for Rebecca.

She sat upright in bed, breathing too fast, lips blue, her chest filled like a balloon. Her grunts woke John, and I could hear Michael and Jen in their rooms calling for us. Like a reflex, we put Rebecca's bathrobe around her and carried her to the car. I drove her to the emergency room at the plan's hospital, ten minutes further away than North City.

When we got there, the triage nurse saw us right away, asked a number of questions about Rebecca's condition, the medications we'd given her, and peak flow meter results. She consulted her computer screen to confirm the medicines Rebecca had been prescribed, checked lab results from our first visit, saw that we'd had an X ray taken three weeks earlier, and moved us to an exam room. I don't remember the doctor's name, but he knew everything about Rebecca when he came in. He checked Rebecca thoroughly and explained that he could order an X ray, but that there was no indication of an infection, no fluids or congested parts of her lungs, and that he was comfortable not putting Rebecca through yet another exam if I was. I told him that I wanted the X ray anyway; that was what we'd done every time in the other hospital, and I wasn't going to go home not knowing whether or not they'd missed something. Besides, I read that health plans make their money by cutting down on needed lab and X-ray studies. The doctor agreed to order the exam and we were led off to the radiology department for the study.

After the results were back, the doctor came back into the exam room and showed us the X ray, which had no evidence of infection, fluid, or consolidation. He explained that we should increase Rebecca's dose of anti-inflammatory medicine for three days, increase the number of puffs on the inhaler for the same period, and see how things go. Already Rebecca's symptoms seemed to be improving because, as he explained what we needed to do, he was helping Rebecca with her inhaler.

"Dr. Foxton and the asthma team work closely with us on the emergency-room staff," he explained. "We all follow the same approach for treating Rebecca and kids like her based on the best science available and our experience with more than 2,000 children." He described how we could have stopped the attack by following the peak flow meter results more closely and changing the medications sooner. He also gave us some suggestions for Rebecca to look for, the early warning signs—how her lungs feel, how her breathing sounds, how hard it is to push the air out, how dry and scratchy her throat feels—that could help her tell John and me that she might be starting an asthma attack.

A couple of weeks later, we tried the parent-group meetings. They turned out to be better than I'd expected. One meeting sticks out in my mind. There were about eleven or twelve of us, mostly mothers like me, but some dads, too. The children met with someone else. We'd already gotten to know each other in earlier gatherings, so we got right down to business. I'm not very good at these things. I don't like talking about myself or my problems, and I get pretty impatient listening to all those other people whine about their situations. But this particular night, one mom said that sometimes she feels like giving up—that she just gets overwhelmed. She said it so simply, not looking for sympathy. Without thinking, I jumped in and agreed with her. I don't know what got into me. All of a sudden, four or five of us were talking about how tired we get, how discouraged we feel, even guilty because our kids have asthma, how crabby we get with our other children and our husbands. John and the other men laughed and agreed with us. Pretty soon we were sharing how we deal with these feelings. One lady said she goes for a walk; another talked about taking time out for a cup of coffee. One mom goes into her bedroom, closes her door, and takes twenty-five—"yes I count them"—deep breaths. And then we talked about how we adjust medicines for our children, how we read the peak flow meter, and how we've each learned to anticipate when something might trigger an asthma attack and what we do with the medicines to stop it.

I don't know where the time went that night, but I can tell you, I came home fired up. The next time I started to feel overwhelmed, I went into my bedroom and took those deep breaths. In fact, once I even called another mother from the group, because we all have each other's phone numbers now, and it turns out we were both feeling pretty much the same thing, so we helped each other just by talking. And the same thing happens with John and the other men. They talked about how they cope, too, and they help each other understand the medications and the peak flow meter. They talked about additional things they'd done in the home to reduce molds and asthma triggers. We support each other, especially after that one night. And I noticed that Rebecca kept talking about "Jim" this and "Carole" that, referring to kids in her group who've been sharing how they deal with their illness.

One night at about seven I got the feeling that Rebecca wasn't doing well. She wasn't wheezing, but her peak flow meter reading was at the edge of the yellow and green zone, and she just didn't seem right. She was complaining about being tired, and she had a runny nose and a scratchy throat. I didn't know whether or not to give her some extra puffs of her medicines. John reminded me about the 800 number, so I called the advice center to see what they could tell me. A nurse answered, introduced herself, listened to my concern, then asked for Rebecca's medical-record number. Once she had the right screen on her computer, she asked me to run through the medicines to see if they were what Dr. Foxton had prescribed. She asked how we were giving the medicines, what we'd given that day, what the peak flow meter reading was, and what Rebecca's symptoms were. Then she advised me to go ahead with extra puffs of both inhalers and watch what happened, and if Rebecca didn't get better, to check with Dr. Wilkensen or Dr. Foxton. Within an hour or so, Rebecca was sleeping peacefully, and she woke up the next morning ready to go to school. I felt like we'd dodged a bullet.

Later in the day, I got a call from Dr. Wilkensen's nurse at the asthma program asking how Rebecca was doing. She had heard from the advice nurse that we'd called the night before. We went over what the advice nurse had suggested, and she agreed that this was the way to care for these situations. Then she asked if I had any questions and confirmed our next appointment.

During our next visit, Rebecca and I met with Paul Guzman, the pharmacist who works with the asthma team. We hadn't met him before but knew about him from the other parents. He's a quiet middle-aged man who helps Dr. Wilkensen, Dr. Foxton, and the asthma team decide what medications work best, and he works with patients and their parents to understand how the medications work, how to take them, and what complications to watch for. He also helps patients get the right laboratory tests to check for complications from the medicines. As the other caregivers did, he went through the medicines with us, but this time, he explained how they work and why they're effective in dealing with asthma. Finally, he told me that all this would be in the medical record shared with the other members of the team, and that he'd be talking with Dr. Foxton that day during the team meeting to bring all the members of the team up to date on how Rebecca was doing.

We've been part of the asthma team for three years now. In fact, John and Rebecca and I have met with the whole team several times, especially when they have new ways to treat asthma or a new drug has just come out that looks promising. We all talk together about whether or not we should be doing anything different for Rebecca. Every now and then, the team lets us know about changes they're making in the care or the way the clinic works; usually it's because they've done some kind of survey—

they're always doing surveys of us!—and have found ways to improve things. I can go to anyone on the team with my questions and concerns, not just Dr. Foxton or Dr. Wilkensen. They all know us and approach Rebecca's care the same way, so we don't get different stories. Besides, they all use the same medical record. So do the other doctors.

Rebecca has learned to take care of her own medicines most of the time. She knows how to read the meter, when to change her medicines, and how to anticipate when she might develop an attack. And when she does get an attack, she doesn't get so scared anymore. She knows what to do to keep it from getting serious. So do we. We're much more confident than we were before. We know what to do most of the time, and we know where to go to find out if we don't. It's great that everyone on the team—the doctors, nurses, health educators, pharmacists—reinforce each other and use the same treatments. I'm confident now that they're basing the treatments on the best science available, because I've checked on the Internet and I've read everything I can, even the articles and studies that Dr. Foxton has given to all of the families in the program.

I was unclear for a long time about how the asthma team and Dr. Wilkensen worked together. Dr. Wilkensen is part of a general pediatrics team, too. When Michael got sick with the flu, we saw a nurse practitioner who practices with Dr. Wilkensen. Another time, we saw Dr. Beremen, a general pediatrician on the team with Dr. Wilkensen. All of them shared the same medical records and used the same approach to care. They'd talked about it, Dr. Wilkensen told me, going over all the scientific literature and deciding how they wanted to treat their patients.

When a child has a more serious problem, like Rebecca does, Dr. Wilkensen brings in the asthma team or another team depending on the diagnosis. "That way we get the most help, and we don't have to do it all ourselves," she explained. "Taking care of tough problems like asthma requires more than just good doctors. Everyone on the team brings something important, and by working together with the patient and the family, we get a lot better results."

What's most surprising is how well Rebecca is doing. In three years, we've had two visits to the emergency room—once just after we started, and once a year ago when she had a bad cold, with coughing and flu symptoms that triggered an asthma attack we couldn't handle at home. She still has attacks, but they're not as bad as they used to be. We know what they look like, and we know what to do to keep them from becoming a real problem. So Rebecca hasn't been hospitalized once in the past five years. She only missed a few days of school last year and this year. She's doing well in her classes, too. She's keeping up with the other children, is comfortable with her friends, and even spends the night now and then with her girlfriend, Amy, a few blocks away from our house. She'd never done that before last year.

She is also playing soccer. I was pretty scared when she came running into the house one day last fall saying she wanted to play. I reminded her what happened when she was six. She explained to me, "That was then, this is now, Mom. I've got things under control." So we let her try it, after talking with the coach to make sure she understood what Rebecca's symptoms are when she's overexerted. We also called Dr. Wilkensen, who suggested that Rebecca take a couple of extra puffs of her inhaler before she exercises if she wants to. The coach promised us that she would pull Rebecca out of the game at the first sign of an attack. John had to go to the first practice; I couldn't stand it. But she did just fine, and the coach seemed to be pretty sensitive to Rebecca's needs. So I was there for the first game. It scared me to death. I don't know if I breathed the whole game! And Rebecca! Good God! She ran up and down the field, shouted at her teammates, took on one large girl on the other team in a scramble for the ball, got shoved to the ground, jumped right up, ran after the bigger girl, and took the ball away from her. At one point she asked the coach to come out, went to her gym bag, pulled out her inhaler, took two quick puffs, rested for about ten minutes, then went back in to finish the game.

John and I recently looked over our expenses from the past couple of years. Our medical bills were almost nonexistent except for the five-dollar copays for all of Rebecca's medicines each time they're filled. They're a lot less than $900 per month, I can assure you! Besides, I've been able to spend more time at my shop, so we're doing better there, too, and as a result, my business partner, Yoshi, has gotten her life together again.

These past few months, I've had a lot more time to spend with Michael and Jennifer. Michael is doing much better in school; in fact, we haven't been called down to school to talk about his problems at all. And Jennifer has come along, too, with better grades, more friends. She's more easygoing at home, too. What a change!

In fact, things are better all round. John has gotten a couple of big cases. His concerns about whether or not he was doing his share in the practice have pretty much disappeared. I've lost fifteen of those twenty-five pounds I gained when Rebecca was so sick. I can focus on my own health a little more now, so I'm eating better and even getting out to walk now and then.

The best thing of all is that last summer we took our first summer family vacation away from town since Rebecca's first asthma attack nearly seven years ago. We went on a road trip through the national parks in Utah and Arizona for two weeks and didn't have a single problem with Rebecca along the way. We had talked to Dr. Wilkensen and Louise to make sure we knew what to do if Rebecca started to get sick. There was always the twenty-four-hour call center, too. So we felt pretty confident we could handle any problems Rebecca might have while we were gone.

Nothing is perfect. I still feel like we get lost sometimes, like they don't know us as well as Dr. Landers did. Not with Dr. Wilkensen or Dr. Foxton or their teams, but with other staff at the clinic. It's pretty big. The waits on the phone can be too long.

I've even hung up a couple of times, I have been so frustrated listening to the recorded messages. But now that John and I know how to find our way around there, the clinic seems a lot more convenient than Dr. Landers's office and all the other doctors we used to go to. And it's a lot better. When I think about how well Rebecca is doing and how much better our life is now, I'm willing to put up with some minor inconveniences along the way.

# 5

# CARE THAT WORKS:
# BEACONS FOR THE FUTURE

THE CARE REBECCA receives from Dr. Wilkensen, Dr. Foxton, and the asthma team has improved the quality of her life and reduced her risk of suffering from severe, life-threatening emergencies. She still has asthma. But now she and her family have the tools to keep the disease under control so she can live a fairly normal life. This is how asthma care is given at Kaiser Permanente. Her medical care could just as easily have been provided by Harvard Vanguard, the Mayo Clinic, Group Health Cooperative, HealthPartners, or a community clinic in Boston or Chicago. The American Lung Association believes this is state-of-the-art care for children and encourages providers and patients to deal with asthma this way because children do so much better than in traditional practices.

It doesn't stop with asthma care. Care given by a physician and a team of medical professionals who work closely with the patient and family works better for a wide range of illnesses. A growing body of research shows this: Patients with chronic illnesses who receive care this way: (1) make fewer emergency-room visits than patients treated in traditional physician practices; (2) are hospitalized less frequently; (3) suffer fewer complications from their disease; (4) are better able to work or maintain the activities of daily living; (5) have greater confidence in their ability to manage their lives and illnesses; and (6) feel more secure with the care they receive. Objective measures of clinical control—laboratory tests, X-ray exams, and physical exam findings—confirm that team-based care achieves better results. Comparisons in rates of immunizations, screening and identification rates for cancers, recovery rates from complex surgery, and the like appear to produce similar results.

In communities throughout the United States and in other parts of the world, we find examples of care that is organized like the care Rebecca received for asthma. These are beacons that guide us as we search for answers to the challenges that medicine faces. They demonstrate that the promise of medical science and technology can be ours at a price we can afford. Our first stop is Boston, Massachusetts.

## Integrated Solutions

### Neighborhood Health Plan, Boston, Massachusetts

Headquartered in an office building east of the north-south freeway in a neighborhood of old warehouses, converted office buildings, and low-income apartments close to the Boston Harbor, Neighborhood Health Plan (NHP) has served mostly low-income, seriously ill Medicaid beneficiaries since the early 1970s through its Community Medical Alliance (CMA) clinical program. Dr. Robert Master, the program's founder and the chief medical officer for NHP, works in a crowded office cluttered with papers and journals and surrounded by exam rooms. Patients and staff move up and down the hall outside his office, phones ring constantly, nurses drop in to let him know that one of his patients is on the line, to ask about a medication, or to tell him that one of his patients said to say hello. The informality and sense of family is pervasive. It's hard not to feel at home. The patients do, joking and smiling with the staff, waving at Dr. Master as they pass by his office, chatting in the waiting rooms like churchgoers at an afternoon social.

Claire Holland* is a CMA patient. At forty-three years old, she is wheelchair bound with cerebral palsy, a disease that imprisons her normal mind in a body unable to coordinate its movements. Severe spasticity prevents her from walking, her arms flail uncontrollably, especially when she's excited, and she grimaces and sometimes drools down the front of her blouse. But Claire is fortunate in some ways: She can speak well enough to be understood if she remembers to take her time. And she is able to work part time at a small plant that employs disabled men and women two blocks from the group home where she's lived for twenty years, ever since she left her family home after completing City College at the age of twenty-three.

Claire suffers the complications of her chronic illness and the effects of being in a wheelchair: osteoarthritis affects her right shoulder, her hips, and her lower back; she has recurring urinary tract infections from sitting in her wheelchair; and periodically she becomes depressed. She takes several medications each day and receives physical therapy twice a week to relieve the stiffness in her joints and back and the crippling effects of her spasticity. Before she discovered CMA ten years ago, she had great difficulty finding doctors to care for her. When she needed care, she had to find someone to drive her to her doctor's appointment, couldn't get on and off an exam table without exhausting herself, and was seen by physicians who had little time to learn about her special needs. So she avoided medical care "like the plague," as she puts it, except for emergencies. As a consequence, she'd never been screened for cervical cancer or breast cancer, she was always running out of her medications, and her osteoarthritis and depression had gotten steadily worse. She was

---

*The names of patients in this chapter have been changed to protect their privacy.

too disabled to work, relying instead on food stamps and welfare to support her limited needs. She rarely ventured out of the group home except to visit her family in south Boston.

The CMA solution for Claire was elegant. The organization enabled her, as it has nearly 900 others with severe, chronic conditions, to get medical care within NHP's overall membership of 135,000 eligible and low-income Medicare and Medicaid individuals. Care is brought to Claire when possible. Professionals teach her to care for herself; help her caregivers learn medical-care basics that she can't handle alone; and help her arrange transportation, renew her Medicaid eligibility, shop, and take care of her personal needs. They also helped her find her job. And they make sure the medical care is accessible and appropriate for her. How is it done?

- *Claire and patients like her are full partners in the care process. They are members of the care team.* Over the past twenty-five years, Dr. Master and his colleagues have learned that successful chronic care starts with successful patients who can take the lead in managing their own conditions.

- *Care is provided by a team of providers: nurse care managers, social workers, nurse practitioners, health educators, physical therapists, pharmacists, and, of course, doctors.* Because the needs are so significant, the coordination issues so complex, and the psychological and social concerns so profound, nurses have primary responsibility for the provision of care. Nurse practitioners are the focal point of the care team. They do comprehensive evaluations when patients first join the program, manage routine medical problems, and respond first to new clinical problems. The physician works with the nurse care manager to manage serious medical conditions in a collegial way rather than in the more traditional top-down relationship. Using the same approach, the physician works with the team to develop an overall plan of care for each patient and provides diagnosis and treatment of complex medical problems and hospital care when required. This difference in style is far from trivial. The medical conditions that Claire and patients like her have can be quite difficult to recognize and treat. The physicians must work hard to stay current with the medical science and new technologies. Every member of the team, though, has a role to play and brings distinct skills and perspectives to the care process.

- *The care process is much broader than the medical care most of us are used to.* Medications and surgery are essential, of course, but care also includes scheduling transportation, helping with Medicare and Medicaid enrollment, arranging grocery delivery, and getting patients to and from their church, synagogue, or mosque. These acts of daily living are often disrupted when illness is severe. Master and his colleagues have seen firsthand that they are essential to a patient's quality of life and sense of well-being, and as a consequence, strongly influence whether or not a patient gets better with medical treatment.

- *The care teams are nested in an organization that provides infrastructure for the teams to work: information systems, links to community support services, and so on.* The organization also helps the teams learn from one another and build information and knowledge that enriches and improves the care process.

Does the CMA program work? Knowing firsthand the fickle nature of public funding for the poor and seriously disabled, and the exhausting professional challenge of meeting the needs of these difficult patients, I am impressed that the program has survived this long. The road to caring for the poor and disabled is littered with broken promises and failed programs in city after city across the country. Our nation's record in meeting the needs of the severely chronically ill with limited resources is not encouraging. The poor and severely disabled often do not vote, and their advocates can be faint voices in the din surrounding other public programs.

NHP is an exception. Dr. Master and his colleagues have shown that the barriers of law, regulation, payment systems, and apathy can be knocked aside and the challenges of caring for this population met effectively and affordably. But as remarkable a survival story as NHP is, even more important is the impact it has had on patients like Claire.

In evaluations conducted in the mid-1990s, researchers found that patients who get their care from NHP work more, experience fewer medical complications, have greater independence, and enjoy a higher quality of life than those with similar conditions treated in traditional settings. They have better control of their medical conditions as measured by visits to emergency rooms, days of hospitalization, days unable to work, and days unable to perform the tasks they usually can do. Patients report that they are healthier, happier, and more satisfied with their care. From a biological point of view, they control their diseases and complications more consistently and effectively and achieve better outcomes as a result. Their care also costs less than the fragmented, uncoordinated, disease-focused, reactive approach that most patients in these situations experience. This not-for-profit health-care system provides care at a premium rate from Medicaid in Massachusetts that is substantially lower than the costs of similar patients in the Massachusetts Medicaid fee-for-service system. Still, the program generates sufficient revenue, after expenses, to invest in critical infrastructure like information technology, clinic upkeep, and new medical technologies. This is a new story for health-care systems caring for these populations, one shared with only a handful of other community care programs around the country that, using similar approaches, have been able to help their patients lead active lives and achieve financial stability for their operations.

NHP isn't just a program for chronically ill and seriously disabled poor people, welfare recipients, the forgotten, and the displaced. The lessons learned at NHP can be applied to any practice serving patients with chronic conditions. The physicians at the Vanguard Medical Group associated with Harvard Pilgrim Health Plan recognized this when they contracted with NHP to care for their patients with advanced HIV/AIDS. NHP gave better care less expensively than Harvard Vanguard could themselves in the more traditional medical model that most of us have used throughout the twentieth century.

## Teams at Work at HealthPartners

HealthPartners, a not-for-profit, community-based, consumer-owned integrated medical-care program serving 700,000 members in the upper Midwest makes extensive use of care teams. They are designed to help patients manage their conditions and to help physicians provide the most effective clinical care that the evidence supports.

Frank Peters, seventy-six years old, is a tough, independent, retired automobile mechanic with congestive heart failure (CHF). Since his condition was first diagnosed in 1995, he has been admitted to the hospital seven times for the disease, four through the emergency room. A pacemaker now helps control his abnormal heart rhythm. Before it was installed, he had a stroke at home, where he has lived alone since his wife died several years ago. Confused and dazed, he was unable to crawl to his phone and call for help for a good seven hours. He wants to continue to live at home and do the things he enjoys: fish with his nephew, hunt deer, gamble at the local casino, and watch wrestling with his buddies on Saturday night.

Immediately following his stroke and the placement of the pacemaker, Mr. Peters enrolled in the HealthPartners Heart Monitor Program, part of a larger effort to provide state-of-the-art care for patients with cardiovascular disease. Twice a day he monitors his weight and answers five questions on a touch pad connected to his phone. If there are any danger signals in the results, a specially trained nurse calls him back. On one occasion, his weight rose several pounds overnight. With questioning, the nurse discovered that Mr. Peters had eaten a high-sodium meal the night before. She took advantage of the opportunity to reinforce earlier messages about the dangers of eating too much salt, especially in processed meats. Mr. Peters knows that if his weight goes up more than three or four pounds overnight, or from one day to the next, he'll get a call. He also knows that if he doesn't report in on schedule, the nurse will get in touch with him to make sure he's okay. It gives him a sense of safety to have this connection and provides the confidence he needs to live independently in spite of his condition.

Of course, there's more to the care Mr. Peters gets than phone-based monitoring. He is part of a comprehensive effort to deal with heart disease. A team of medical professionals has worked with patients with congestive heart failure to determine what patients need from their interactions with the medical team. In addition, 966 patients from ten HealthPartners Medical Group clinics were surveyed to determine: (1) perceptions of current health; (2) perceptions of care compared to a year earlier; (3) emotional and physical function status; (4) access to care; and (5) patient motivation and education relating to salt intake, disease process, and daily weights. Education and support programs were developed based in part on these results. Clinical care is designed by a team of clinicians and researchers that includes doctors, nurses, health educators, epidemiologists, pharmacists, and dietitians. Regular quality improvement has been undertaken since the program was launched in 1997. Physician and staff educational programs have focused on bringing the science and the tools to all professionals who care for patients with CHF.

The program employs a variety of care tools. Group visits are used in some clinics. Educational and skill-building materials have been developed specifically for patients with CHF. Home health nurses, outpatient and inpatient nurse case managers, dietitians, and a wide variety of specialty services are integrated into the care process. Patients are identified and tracked using an automated chronic-disease registry to enable staff, especially primary-care providers and cardiologists, to maintain contact with their patients. The registry also helps providers know when follow-up studies are required and who should be contacted when medications need to be changed. Pharmacists, with access to all critical clinical information about medications, work with medical professionals and the patients to help them with medication schedules and doses and to avoid complications. They also partner with the physicians to make sure patients receive appropriate laboratory testing to check for complications of medications. Patients like Mr. Peters have access to electronic, home-based monitoring systems that enable patients to send weights and other symptom information to nurses twice a day. Special written and video-based educational materials are provided to patients in the program, as is access to the "Partners for Better Health" phone line, with phone-based counseling and prerecorded educational tapes on diet and healthy lifestyles, including exercise, smoking cessation, stress management, and other conditions.

The results of the program are impressive. In the three-year period from 1997–2000, hospital admissions for patients with congestive heart failure dropped 42 percent, and emergency-room visits were down by 20 percent. The proportion of patients on an ACE inhibitor, a medication important for reducing the frequency of complications in patients with CHF, has increased significantly. Patients report improvements in their self-rated general health as a result of the program as well.

HealthPartners uses similar approaches for a number of conditions. The teams focus on giving patients:

- The tools they need to manage their conditions with help from medical professionals.

- Medical care based on the best medical science currently available.

- Care and support that bring together the skills, perspectives, and experiences of medical professionals on a care team.

- Access to their medical providers using up-to-date information and communications technologies.

- Information-technology support that enables physicians and other medical professionals to share critical clinical information about them and track their progress.

- Care that is continuously improved as a result of systematic assessment of performance and continuous surveys of patients and families to determine what is working for them and what is not.

The physicians are the leaders on the team, providing clinical expertise and patient monitoring essential for complicated patients like Mr. Peters. The doctors, in turn, are surrounded by a team of highly qualified and trained professionals. And the HealthPartners organization provides support for the development of educational materials, surveys, and data management and analysis, and supplies the capital for information technology and medical technologies. Beyond the impressive results for Mr. Peters and patients like him with CHF, HealthPartners achieves superb results for its members. Patients and members respond with a high level of satisfaction and loyalty. The proportion of members who leave HealthPartners when offered a chance to do so each year at open enrollment is one of the lowest in health care: about 2 percent per year.

## Good Doctors and Good Systems:
## Premier Health Partners in Dayton, Ohio

Premier Health Partners in Dayton, Ohio, includes more than 100 physician practices, two hospitals, a long-term care facility, and a home health agency. The physicians, like our fictional Dr. Landers, are independent. The leaders of Premier Health Partners decided to change the models of care for chronic illness because these conditions had become a major part of what their member physicians dealt with day in and day out. The leaders started with the assumption that the physicians in the network were motivated to be good doctors but lacked the support systems and tools they needed to practice up-to-date chronic-disease care. Starting with adult diabetes, the clinical leaders developed a comprehensive set of tools and system changes:

- New tracking forms

- Educational materials

- Clinical guidelines

- Documentation forms

- Reminder letters for patients

- Home-care forms for patients to help with self-management and monitoring

• Educational programs for patient groups

The physician and nurse directors of Premier's quality program visited every physician in the network to share the materials and answer questions. This "academic detailing," as they called it (after the doctor-to-doctor selling that drug companies call "drug detailing"), was designed to provide each physician the chance to work with the Premier team to determine how to incorporate the program into his or her practice. Special attention was given to the physician skeptics. Initially, only a small core of doctors joined the effort. Within two years, every physician in the network had incorporated the guidelines and tools into their practices. Now the quality leaders are expanding the program to cardiac disease and asthma and to basic preventive services.

**Results.** The results are encouraging. In 1999, at the outset of the program, only 42 percent of adult diabetics had blood-sugar levels that were considered under control. Within two years, the number had improved to 70 percent. In 1997, physicians were checking blood-sugar levels (hemoglobin A1c) twice a year only 67 percent of the time; by 2001, the number had risen to 90 percent. Proper foot exams for diabetic ulcers, annual urine protein measures, and the use of ACE inhibitors in patients with positive proteins have increased 17 percent, 26 percent, and 42 percent, respectively. The results are also accompanied by a strong business case. The leaders studied patient medical-care use at the outset of the project and two years later. The number of visits that patients made to their doctors and emergency rooms for problems related to diabetes fell dramatically as a result of the tight control of blood sugar, excellent education, and careful monitoring.

**Summary.** Physicians in the Premier network were able to provide high-quality care similar to what has been observed at the Neighborhood Health Plan, HealthPartners, or Kaiser Permanente because:

- Patients are directly involved in their own care, which builds confidence and skills, and have the tools to manage their conditions with the help of their physicians.

- Physicians are supported in their search for the best practices and in developing ways to incorporate those practices into their daily routines.

- Teams of care professionals work with the physician and patient to provide skills, perspectives, and tools that the doctor cannot provide alone.

- Support for doctors and patients and other medical professionals includes:

  - Education
  - Guidelines
  - Practice tools
  - Information-technology support
  - Reinforcement

## Building the Organization: Intermountain Health Care, Salt Lake City, Utah

Intermountain Health Care (IHC) has been a leader in quality and innovation in medical care for more than twenty-five years. The organization employs 400 physicians who practice in almost 100 outpatient clinics that IHC owns and operates. Another 800 community physicians are closely affiliated with IHC. IHC operates its own Health Plan and a not-for-profit Preferred Provider Organization and provides coverage for 400,000 people. The organization is also deeply involved with the state Medicaid program and provides about 50 percent of the Medicare services in the state.

Author Michael Millensen, whose book *Demanding Medical Excellence* chronicles the development of the quality movement in medical care, highlights the innovative work in quality management that has occurred at IHC. Clinical and program leaders draw heavily on patient perspectives to design clinical services and evaluate the quality and responsiveness of the care. Dr. Brent James, the surgeon leader of the program's quality-improvement and research efforts, has also worked with clinical and administrative leaders to incorporate principles of production design into the reorganization of hospital-based services.

When it came time to redesign the neonatal intensive care unit at the 460-bed Utah Valley Regional Medical Center in Provo, Utah, Dr. Stephen Minton, director of neonatology, asked mothers and fathers whose babies had required intensive care to help design the new service. Working together, the team mapped out a clinical program and a physical layout that would support close parent-child relationships. A similar approach was used to redesign ambulatory surgical services for the Urban Central Region of IHC, which consists of the flagship LDS Hospital in Salt Lake City, two smaller hospitals, and a series of associated stand-alone surgery centers.

Dr. James and his colleagues also give patients a direct say in the evaluation of clinical care, the assessment of the support services they receive, and the design of new services and facilities. The leaders believe that if medical care does not meet patient needs or respect individual choices and desires, it is not high-quality care no matter how skilled the physicians and other medical professionals might be. The IHC leaders do not neglect the support systems for clinical delivery. They have invested heavily in an automated clinical information system that provides pharmacy and laboratory results, clinical notes, and decision support for clinicians. One measure of the value of this investment, from a patient's point of view, is this: IHC is developing the capacity for patients to "own" their medical records, with access to and use of those records on a daily basis. Another measure is that physicians with access to the clinical information system are far more likely than their colleagues to provide their patients with care that is consistent with the most up-to-date and effective medical science.

The close relationship between patients and doctors and the organization seen at IHC is also found at Group Health Cooperative of Puget Sound in Washington State and Idaho. This consumer cooperative provides medical coverage and care for 800,000 members located throughout Washington State and western Idaho. Consumer councils and committees ensure that patient and members views are included in decisions about organizational strategy, investment choices, clinical services, and medical effectiveness. HealthPartners, the consumer cooperative mentioned earlier, also makes extensive use of consumer assessments and input to design and evaluate its services.

## Whatcomb County, Washington

Peace Health System, a Catholic hospital network serving the Pacific Northwest, is trying to bring together the players in Whatcomb County, located north of Seattle, Washington. Ten years ago, the hospital system leaders worked with community physicians, public health officials, and local business owners to build a Community Health Information Network to identify and track patients with chronic illnesses as they received care in the county. Now the group is focused on actually putting together the fragmented pieces of medical care into a coherent system for patients with chronic conditions. Two local Indian tribes have been added to the original group, in addition to the county's faith-based institutions, the two primary health insurers (Group Health Cooperative and Regents, the Blue Cross organization), and local government officials. Funded by Peace Health System and in-kind support from a number of other players, the effort is designed to:

- Enable patients to have full access to their own clinical information.

- Provide access to clinical records approved for providers any time of the day or night.

- Provide case-management services to help patients move from one part of the system to another as their care requires.

- Ensure that patients receive care that is based on the best that medical science has to offer.

Physicians in the community will have access to clinical information twenty-four hours a day from their offices or homes. Already, those in the project can order laboratory tests and pharmaceuticals online and have access to registries of their patients with chronic conditions. Patients have been involved in the design of the system throughout the process and participate in the governance of the project with other professionals and local leaders.

John Hayward, executive vice president of Peace Health, describes the process as an uphill battle. As he explains:

- Fee-for-service reimbursement systems often don't reward doctors and hospitals for doing the right thing.

- Keeping all the players engaged in the slow process of consensus building is difficult.

- Staying focused on the patients and their needs is difficult when day-to-day conflicts among the players flare up.

- Decision-making and management of the effort is difficult when so many people and organizations are involved.

Hayward's board is worried that the large investment they are making will not pay dividends. They also worry that keeping people healthy and out of the hospital will hurt their bottom line so much that they won't be able to continue their other community-service activities. Nonetheless, Hayward and his colleagues, including the project directors, Nancy Bitting, Dr. Jim Scott, and Dr. Mark Pierson, are committed to seeing this concept through. They believe deeply that it is the only way patients will be able to gain some control over the conditions they have.

To keep focused on the task at hand, those engaged in the work interact regularly with patients with chronic illness. Hayward relates a case that has guided his work, the story of a forty-year-old mother with diabetes and heart disease. She takes insulin twice a day, her right leg was amputated below the knee because of diabetic ulcers that resulted from poor circulation, and she's losing her eyesight. During a town meeting to discuss the project, she said she has "an internist to take care of my regular problems, an endocrinologist to take care of my diabetes, a vascular surgeon to take care of my circulatory problems, a cardiologist to treat my heart disease, and an ophthalmologist to take care of my eye problems." The doctors do not communicate with one another; each one keeps his own records and does things his own way. The patient has to put it all together for herself and make sense of the confusion because the medical-care system is not designed to. "You people need to get it together," the woman told the professionals and community leaders. Hayward agrees.

### The Esther Project: Jönköping County, Sweden

"Esther" is eighty-seven years old. She lives alone and suffers from congestive heart failure and an abnormal heart rhythm.

Her daughter lives nearby and looks in on her several times a week. Her picture shows a kindly gray-haired woman, wrinkled with age, looking directly at the camera. In reality, the woman in the picture is an actress, and "Esther" is a fiction, a persona. But she's nevertheless the driving force behind a major overhaul of the medical-care delivery system in Jönköping County in central Sweden. This is a county with a population of 300,000 people served by three hospitals and a host of physicians employed by the government. There are no private physicians in Sweden. In an effort to make the needs of patients seem more immediate to those who make abstract decisions, medical leaders created Esther and organized their project around her. Their focus was to redesign medical services so that people like Esther, with conditions that require several sources of support from the medical-care system, could obtain care more smoothly and easily. When the medical professionals and officials talk about redesigning medical care, they refer to Esther. Her picture is on the wall at meetings and adorns many of the planning documents. Their work revolves around how to improve things for her, and they are constantly asking the question, "How can we make this easier for Esther?"

The professionals and administrators in Jönköping County have made significant changes in the organization of medical care. As in many communities across the developed world, in Jönköping County before the Esther Project each doctor's office, hospital, emergency room, and community-support agency worked in its own world. Doctors jealously guarded their practices and their patients (even though they were salaried government employees). Medical leaders, such as Dr. Mats Bojestig, the county health officer, brought the players together, championing the idea that by working collaboratively, care could be improved for Esther. Bojestig rarely failed to mention Esther in his discussions with other medical professionals and community leaders. He and other leaders provided critical resources to help the teams that worked on improving Esther's care.

Teams were made up of people from among the medical professions. They focused on speeding up the transfer of important information from one provider to another and helping patients access needed care across the system with fewer delays. Leaders routinely asked whether or not the "flow" through the system had been improved for Esther, examining both quantitative and qualitative measures to test the observations.

One improvement has been in the coordination between emergency and home care. Visiting nurses have worked with emergency-room professionals to identify why patients visited the emergency rooms and what home-based care and other interventions might reduce the reliance on emergency care among the elderly. The result was:

- Better in-home tracking

- More frequent in-home contacts

- Better education for patients in self-management and diagnosis to enable them to adjust their treatments and recognize symptoms more readily

- Better-informed families

- More phone consultations

- Better chronic-pain management

In addition, patients with chronic conditions such as congestive heart failure, high blood pressure, and obesity have been taught to monitor vital information about weight and blood pressure. Relations among the professionals involved in eldercare have improved as well. Information moves more readily among visiting nurses, health educators, and physicians and between the institutions involved in providing care. Always, as efforts are made to improve this part of the system or integrate that set of activities for patients, Esther's picture and story are the centerpiece. "What does Esther need?" is the question that helps people move from dry and conflicting statistical stories to real human solutions.

Laurel Simmons, a member of the Institute for Healthcare Improvement staff in Boston, Massachusetts, is working with the Jönköping County officials on the project. She says that when project leaders get lost in the data or the traditional culture of medicine, Esther's face and story helps people break through the barriers. The Esther Project has in effect put a real patient at the center of the effort. Doing so has enabled the project leaders and the work teams to cut through the impediments that often bring well-intended efforts like these to a premature and unsatisfactory conclusion. Strong leaders, organizational resources, and work teams are enabling the changes to happen. Esther and people like her in Jönköping County are the beneficiaries.

# Tools

As medical professionals continue to search for better ways to provide care to patients, a wide range of tools have emerged that represent important new pieces in the puzzle.

### The Shared Decision-Making Model

One cornerstone of Claire Holland's care at Community Medical Alliance in Boston was to help her gain the confidence to make decisions for herself and provide her own care whenever possible. Some researchers have taken this objective a step further using technology to help patients make informed decisions about their treatment choices for common conditions.

Jim Noland, a stockbroker in Denver, Colorado, is nearing sixty years of age and has begun to experience what he and his male friends call "the old man's urge." He wakes up two or three times a night to urinate, has to go immediately when the urge hits him; urinates in stops and starts when he goes; and, most embarrassing of all, has begun to dribble, discoloring his underwear and sometimes staining his pants. He suspects this is a condition called benign prostatic hyperplasia (BPH), an enlargement of the prostate gland, which is located near the bladder, resulting in a partial blockage of the tube that drains the bladder through the penis. This benign condition is something most aging men experience, and it sometimes coincides with a malignant tumor. At least two of Jim's friends have had surgery for prostate cancer; several others have had treatments for BPH because of similar symptoms. One friend recently had some of his prostate removed surgically in a procedure called "transurethral resection of the prostate," known usually by the shorthand "TURP."

Jim's primary-care physician confirms Jim's hunch. His prostate is enlarged to twice its normal size but there is no evidence of cancer. Faced with unpleasant symptoms, many physicians prefer to refer someone like Jim to a surgeon, usually a urologist who specializes in surgical treatment of problems of the urinary tract and kidneys. TURPs are common: Rates vary widely among communities, according to the Dartmouth Atlas annual study, using Medicare data, from 3 to 20 surgeries for every 1,000 men at risk after correcting for age. The average is around 12 to 14 surgeries per 1,000 men at risk; it is one of the most commonly performed procedures on men. But Jim is fortunate. His physicians are part of an innovative program developed at Harvard and Dartmouth Medical Schools by Drs. Albert Mulley, John Wennberg, Mike Barry, and Jack Fowler. Using an interactive web-based program, supplemented with an in-depth videotape that Jim can view in the doctor's office or take home to view in private, the doctors provide Jim with information about his choices for treatment. Surgery, Jim learns, is likely to relieve symptoms quite a bit but carries a significant risk of complications that may be for him more unpleasant than those he's now experiencing. These include ejaculation backward into the bladder, or, more rarely, difficulty achieving an erection. Another option, medication, doesn't relieve symptoms nearly as much as surgery does but also carries the risk of side effects.

Jim works through the program, studies the odds compiled by the researchers from studies published in reputable medical journals, and, together with his wife, decides that he'd rather live with his symptoms than subject himself to the risks of surgery or the possible side effects of medication. In making this decision, Jim joins many men who opt to live with their symptoms once they understand their choices. In the original study of this approach in the early 1990s at Group Health Cooperative of Puget Sound and Kaiser Permanente in Colorado, TURP surgery rates fell 40 percent. Prostate surgery rates at both medical-care organizations were already significantly lower than average. Given information and choices, patients were even more conservative than doctors in these two organizations. The trick is to provide clear, useful information presented in a way that can be understood by nonclinicians. Also, the choice must be the patient's. Some, like Jim, will choose a wait-and-see approach, whereas others may prefer to get it over with through surgery or medical intervention.

Mulley, Wennberg, and their colleagues have developed similar decision-support programs for patients suffering from prostate cancer, breast cancer, back pain, coronary artery disease, and several other conditions. They've also developed a simple videotape to help men decide whether or not to be screened for prostate cancer with a blood test that measures prostate specific antigen (PSA) levels. The impact is instructive. In general, when patients are given choices they trust, they select less invasive alternatives and are more willing to live with symptoms longer rather than risk unpleasant complications.

The researchers at Harvard and Dartmouth, and others who have developed and evaluated similar decision-support tools, have made several more interesting observations. They found, for example, that when given the chance, the patient can and will use these support tools. Moreover, patients who have the opportunity to choose are more comfortable with the care they receive. Finally, because the choice is so often conservative, care given this way is less expensive than the more invasive and riskier alternatives commonly recommended by physicians. Approximately 100 decision aids have been described in the medical literature. About 40 percent have been updated to include current scientific evidence and remain available for use. Mulley, Wennberg, and colleagues have produced 40 percent of the shared decision-making tools now available in the United States and Canada, and they continue to expand the number of conditions for which complete decision-support programs have been developed.

### Supporting the Patient: Group Visits

Another way to enable patients to become partners in their care is through patient group visits. Southern Alabama Medical School uses this approach for adult diabetics who receive care in the Family Practice Residency program. So do Kaiser Permanente, the Mayo Clinic, and a host of others. The format is simple. Patients are usually grouped according to:

- Their condition (diagnosis)

- Their health status (for example, elderly with chronic conditions; patients seeking same-day appointments for urgent problems; etc.)

- Their impending surgery (hip replacement, for example)

They meet regularly with their physician, and often a nurse, and periodically with other medical-team members, depending on the condition (for example, a patient with diabetes might meet with a podiatrist, a nutritionist, and a pharmacist).

The sessions are organized to:

- Provide specific information and develop skills for self-management

- Answer questions

- Share solutions among the patients

We've been taught about the importance of our one-on-one relationship with our physician. Yet patients who participate in group care report a closer and more effective personal relationship with their physician than patients in "normal" physician-patient interactions. They also use care less frequently and achieve greater clinical control of their conditions than their counterparts in traditional practices. There is something therapeutic about these get-togethers; the support within the group for one another is part of it. The group also provides a safe place for patients to ask questions that they might be reluctant to ask in a brief one-on-one visit with their doctor.

## Clinical Information: Kaiser Permanente

Kaiser Permanente, like IHC and other medical-care organizations, has made a solid commitment to the development and use of clinical information systems to support physicians. Kaiser Permanente (KP) is the largest private integrated medical-care system in the world, taking care of more than 8 million members in nine states and Washington, D.C. Nearly 11,000 physicians practice in eight independent KP medical groups. The program employs over 120,000 professionals and support staff in hospitals, outpatient, and administrative centers throughout the country. By 2006, every physician and clinician in the program will have access to a fully automated clinical information system that provides automated medical records and guidance. It won't matter where the patient is cared for—office, home, phone call, emergency room, or hospital—the critical information will be available online. The KP Online system, designed for and by clinicians, incorporates the guidelines for care developed by the Care Management Institute, a Kaiser Permanente resource in which clinicians and scientists review the world's scientific literature to determine what approaches will produce the best results.

The cost of fully implementing the system throughout the KP program is staggering in 2000 dollars, an estimated $1.5 billion to $2 billion, and another $1.5 billion in maintenance in the first several years thereafter. The results, similar to those observed at Intermountain Health Care, are remarkable in terms of better, more consistent care for patients. KP leaders believe that information technology is the glue for the care system, bringing the teams of doctors and medical professionals and patients together into an integrated whole. In fact, the leaders believe that modern medicine cannot be practiced effectively and safely without information-technology support. The clinicians who have been involved in using the prototypes in KP's Northwest and Colorado regions for the past decade would agree. The most common comment among physicians, once they have learned to use the automated clinical information system, is that they would never go back to practicing the old way. When the clinical information system is combined with the member-focused KP Online mentioned earlier, KP will be able to offer patients a complete suite of automated support functions.

## The Virtual Group: MDserve

Dr. Roger Shultz specializes in internal medicine. He and ten colleagues formed Memorial Clinical Associates (MCA), a primary-care group practice in Houston, Texas, more than fifteen years ago. More recently, Shultz also helped create a larger independent practice association made up of more than 100 physicians of different specialties practicing in the Houston area. Originally, the intent of the larger association was to give doctors more clout to deal with the managed-care insurance companies. Now the association has begun to shift its focus to helping member physicians improve their practice management and work more effectively together. Shultz's smaller group has pioneered the development of a new practice-management information technology in collaboration with Michael Barron and Khanh Phi. Michael, formerly a leader in the information-technology department of British Petroleum, and Khanh Phi, a gifted software designer, first built a practice-management system that was licensed to physicians throughout the country. As technology advanced, they rewrote the entire suite of software services to function online on an Application Service Provider (ASP). This approach enables physicians to have access to the software without the large licensing fees or the recurrent fees and hassle of having to upgrade the software as new versions are produced. Instead, in the ASP model, a host houses the common software, provides it to each subscriber practice online, and upgrades it as new versions emerge. Users pay a monthly subscription, or "user," fee. In the case of MDserve, the fees are far lower than the cost of the traditional software licenses: $100 per user per month versus $5,000–$25,000 per licensed software package. Physicians and their practice managers can use the MDserve software to handle routine tasks in their practices such as billing, coding, benefits checking, scheduling, and the like.

More exciting and unique, however, is the decision to build the software to enable physicians to work together in what has been called by some a "virtual group." The intent is to provide the communication infrastructure that facilitates patient referrals to specialists and to share critical sociodemographic and clinical information among physicians and other medical providers. Fully deployed, the system can also function as the backbone for other elements of group practice: order-entry for laboratory and X-ray work, prescriptions, and follow-up; shared decision-making support for clinical care; and case reviews for quality and safety improvement. Basic practice administration and management are the first building blocks in the process. By making easily used and well-tested software available to practicing physicians at relatively low cost, MDserve will provide a foundation across multiple practices on which clinical applications can be built. Eventually, according to John Romer, CEO of MDserve, the ASP-based software will be the information-technology engine for bringing physicians and other medical professionals together into virtual groups. Independent physicians who are linked electronically can provide patients with many of the benefits that formally organized medical groups have while retaining the benefits of small, intimate practice settings.

MDserve has enjoyed modest success to date after entering the crowded, highly competitive, fragmented field of practice-management software years ago. Recent agreements with Federally Qualified Health Centers in Arizona, New Mexico, and New York promise wider adoption of this approach. A growing subscriber base in the Southeast and Midwest of independent practice associations, smaller medical groups like Dr. Shultz's, and individual physician practices is encouraging. If it is successful, MDserve will be an important tool for bringing greater coherence to the fragmented delivery of care that most patients now receive. Dr. Shultz believes in the approach. He and his colleagues have invested in the company, provide important practical and technical guidance to the software developers, and serve as a demonstration site for its use.

## Online Services

Many medical-care organizations are experimenting with web-based or electronic communications systems to link patients more closely and conveniently to their medical care. One example is KP Online, the Kaiser Permanente members-only Internet link mentioned earlier. This password-protected service enables members to make appointments, refill prescriptions, learn about their health, obtain advice from nurses and pharmacists, and join discussions moderated by Kaiser Permanente clinicians. One woman was able to request her appointment on the web from Delhi, India, where she was vacationing with her family. She'd forgotten to arrange school physical exams for her three children. So she requested the appointments online, and while she was at it, made a routine gynecology appointment for herself, refilled her prescriptions so they could be sent by mail to her home when she returned, and signed off. Had she needed to, she could have sent a message to a nurse or pharmacist and received a response in twenty-four hours, or participated in one of the many message boards with other members.

Now serving nearly 600,000 members, the KP Online service will soon be available to 8.2 million members across the country. Additional features will be added to the website in the coming years. This platform will serve as the entry point for an expanded home-based communications system that will enable patients to send their clinical data electronically, receive interpretations and support from medical professionals, and adjust treatments accordingly. It will also be the mechanism by which members who wish to do so can access their own medical records.

Home-based monitoring and care technologies represent a rapidly expanding set of choices for patients. One clever device, developed by engineers at Georgia Tech and approved by the Food and Drug Administration in the late 1990s, is directed to homebound patients with chronic illnesses. The device can handle eight separate monitoring measures. All the data are sent, sometimes as often as four times a day, through the device by telephone to a team of nurses. Patients can also interact with their nurse by video monitor and can obtain video-feed health-information classes on demand. The nurses are connected to the patients' physicians, who provide clinical backup and advice to the nurses. Currently in use in the Mayo Clinic in Florida and in parts of the Midwest, the integrated home-monitoring device with visiting nurse hook-ups has proven helpful in caring for seriously ill patients. Productivity of nurses has risen dramatically.

Most significant, patients are able to live at home longer and suffer fewer complications from their illnesses.

## Preparing for the Unthinkable: Bioterrorism

We return to HealthPartners in Minneapolis, where clinical leaders have combined the best of clinical practice and information technology to provide surveillance data to enable public health officials to determine whether or not bioterrorist attacks have occurred. The HealthPartners solution also provides a glimpse of how clinical surveillance data can help improve medical care for patients under normal circumstances. As widely reported in the wake of the anthrax outbreaks in 2001, HealthPartners uses clinical encounter logs, stripped of individual names and information to protect confidentiality, to track disease incidence. Information is provided by HealthPartners researchers to the disease surveillance unit of the Minnesota Department of Health. These collaborative efforts between HealthPartners researchers and state public health officials are supported by the federal Centers for Disease Control and Prevention (CDC). As information emerges from the CDC or local and state health departments about possible bioterrorist activity, it can be passed on to the HealthPartners clinicians and researchers. They, in turn, can monitor their information to determine if a problem is developing.

# Identifying the Examples

Several organizations identify the innovations that help us understand what our medical care might look like in the future.

## The Institute for Healthcare Improvement

The Institute for Healthcare Improvement is led by Dr. Donald M. Berwick, president and CEO, a pediatrician who became involved in medical quality more than twenty years ago at the Harvard Community Health Plan (now Harvard Pilgrim). A decade ago he left Harvard Community to found the institute, where he and his colleagues have emerged as leaders in the nation's quality-improvement and patient-safety efforts. He and his associates:

- Identify innovative programs to improve care quality and patient safety from around the country, and now the world.

- Systematically share the experiences with others.

- Identify critical lessons and generalizations from these experiences.

- Use these applied solutions and lessons to encourage others to change.

Conferences, training programs, publications, consultants, a rich network of contacts, and an innovative "Breakthrough Series" are used to help transfer best practices. A focus on successful, continuous quality-improvement techniques adapted from other industries helps medical-care institutions enhance their care in a highly disciplined way. In their "Pursuit of Perfection" project, funded by the Robert Wood Johnson Foundation, the institute has selected a small number of health-care organizations and initiatives to learn together to achieve quality and safety levels that are similar to those in superior organizations and companies outside of medicine. Berwick is a medical Johnny Appleseed, spreading seeds of innovation and learning everywhere he goes. He has been a leader in bringing the tools that other industries use to improve their quality to medical care.

## Improving Chronic Illness Care (ICIC)

Dr. Edward Wagner, a specialist in internal medicine and a well-known health-services researcher, leads this effort, which is also funded by the Robert Wood Johnson Foundation. Located in

Seattle at the MacColl Institute for Healthcare Innovation (Group Health Cooperative of Puget Sound), the project is focused on identifying and transferring best practices for the care of people with chronic conditions. Since its inception four years ago, the program has found dozens of practices with useful innovations and worked with more than 400 organizations to transfer the lessons to them. Wagner and his colleagues have developed the evidence that compares alternative approaches for chronic care management. From the combination of real-world experiences and careful analysis, they have created a compelling and urgent case.

Wagner and his colleagues argue that four elements are required for the best care:

- A patient who is capable of sharing in medical decisions and managing much of the care for himself or herself.

- A practice team made up of prepared and well-organized medical professionals and support staff.

- An organization that provides critical support services to the teams and patients.

- Links to the community for other services not routinely available within the traditional acute medical-care system.

## Health Research and Educational Trust (HRET)

HRET, associated with the American Hospital Association, has a sixty-year history of conducting research and pursuing developments that improve medical care across the country. Under the leadership of Mary Pittman, its president for nearly a decade, the organization has explored innovative approaches that link providers, institutions, community resources, and community leaders to create better care for patients and families. Its focus is not exclusively on chronic illness or complex medical conditions, although many of the programs its staff has helped to develop affect patients with these concerns. The staff's work spans medical conditions and often includes the underserved and disenfranchised populations within a community. Their approach includes:

- Building networks among communities to facilitate sharing of best practices.

- Evaluating the impact of innovations in care-delivery system organization and practice.

- Educating the broader medical community about their findings.

- Introducing into public policy their experience and research findings.

One of HRET's major initiatives is the national Community Care Network (CCN) Demonstration Program, carried out in partnership with the American Hospital Association, the Catholic Health Association of the United States, and the VHA Health Foundation. With funding from the W. K. Kellogg Foundation and the Duke Endowment, HRET and its partners identified twenty-five communities across the country focused on improving the health—broadly defined—of their populations. The communities range from urban to suburban and rural and include the wealthy as well as the poor.

A central finding of the demonstration project has been that to achieve the greatest impact on quality and affordability for patients, the medical providers, institutions, and community-support organizations have to work together in a coordinated, integrated manner. Moreover, planning for improved care is enhanced when there is accurate data available to describe what people are facing in terms of health problems, how they receive care when they need it, and what they expect and want from their care. When this information is collected for a community, it becomes a powerful tool for making critical changes in the way care is financed and organized and how providers and institutions can be held accountable.

These three organizations have set out to show how today's medicine can incorporate the most innovative practices across the nation. As leaders in this relatively new effort, they already have compiled a rich library of examples and studies and are promoting the most advanced understanding of what medicine needs to become. They share a conviction that solutions lie beyond traditional medical practice. They also search for the tools and perspectives outside of medicine that can help medicine improve. By so doing, they help us find the beacons and understand the path these illuminate.

# 6

# OUTSIDE THE WALLS:
# SOME LESSONS FROM OTHER
# INDUSTRIES

I CANNOT BEGIN to count the number of times someone has argued that lessons from other industries do not apply to medicine because taking care of patients is "different," or "unique." This is like suggesting that because the Moon and Mars orbit different celestial bodies, we shouldn't use the lessons of the Moon shots to inform the space probes to Mars. What happens between a doctor and a patient is vital; healing and caring occur most successfully in intimate and special exchanges between clinician and patient. Medical decisions and support must meet the special and unique needs of each patient. But to insist that medicine can learn nothing from the experiences of other industries or that these critical elements of the healing process exempt medicine from the lessons others can teach is to build walls that lock those inside in perpetual shadow. Trapped in this semi-darkness, medical professionals shuffle in circles, dancing their arthritic dance without end, hidden from sources of light that can lead them from their self-imposed prison.

The work of others in several areas can help medical care respond to the challenges it faces while maintaining, even enhancing, the central focus on the individual patient and the relationship between patient and clinician. These strategies include the use of *teams* to deal with complex problems and *systems* to support, enhance, and assure individual *knowledge and skills*. Specific operational design and management tools that have had a powerful impact on cost and quality can be adapted to medical care: *production-design processes* to integrate the individuals and sites involved in the care of complex and chronic illnesses; *mass-customization techniques* to marry mass production and individual choice; and *quality-improvement techniques* to improve care and affordability. Finally, others outside of medicine have advanced our understanding of the design of *organizations* to support individual and team-based initiatives, day-to-day operations, and consistent responsiveness to individual customers.

## Teams

### The Issue

Modern medicine requires ensembles, even orchestras sometimes, to deliver most of what it now can offer. But many clinicians, and especially physicians, follow their own scores, isolate themselves in their own sound- and sight-proof booths, are trained as soloists, and believe they conduct the orchestra. As a patient, the more complex your illness or condition is, the more likely you will be treated by several physician specialists and interact with an increasing number of medical professionals and support staff. A person who has heart surgery may interact with as many as 250 different medical professionals in the course of the hospital stay. An elderly patient who suffers from a stroke may see a dozen different doctors and ten times that many other medical professionals during a typical five-day stay in the hospital. When you add the care received before and after the hospital stay, the number of people you depend on grows even larger.

The sicker you are, the more critical it is to take advantage of the special training and experience of the doctor, the nurse, the pharmacist, the nutritionist, the health educator, and anyone else who can help you. The doctors and other medical professionals must work together, use the same basic approaches, and share what they've learned about you so that they can continue to improve the care you receive. You don't want advice to conflict, explanations to confuse, or treatments to interact to cause complications. You don't want to be victimized by medical mistakes when you move from one caregiver to the next or from one site to the next. Nor do you want critical information you give one caregiver to be unavailable to the others when they need it.

Yet, with the exception of innovations like the ones described in the previous chapter, medicine is doing little to work in patient care teams. Even where teams have been used, only tentative steps have been taken to develop an understanding of how to employ them, how to form and support them, and how to help teams work with other teams.

Contrast this with the many industries where virtually all day-to-day work involves teams of one sort or another at every level of the organization. Author John Katzenbach writes in *The Wisdom of Teams* that teams are the basic organizational building block for most firms. Here's what other industries can teach us.

## Example One: Agilent Technologies

Agilent Technologies is a global manufacturer of precision measurement instruments for the technology industries. Until 1999, when it became an independent company, it was part of Hewlett-Packard, representing the core of the original company founded sixty years ago by Bill Hewlett and Dave Packard. It has taken some of the old HP culture with it, adding important new approaches to create a dynamic high-technology corporation that provides leading-edge measurement solutions to companies in the computing, communications, and life-science industries. Teamwork is a cornerstone of both the original HP company and the new Agilent. Teams, made up of people from different backgrounds, are used to address a range of challenges in both companies. They work on everything from broad company strategy to day-to-day operations.

The first task that Agilent President and CEO Ned Barnholt faced when he was chosen to lead Agilent was to build his leadership team. He knew that the success of the new company depended on the quality of people around him. Barnholt doesn't believe in the John Wayne myth of management in which decisions are made by an all-knowing, all-powerful CEO-potentate. After reviewing a number of potential candidates, he selected his chief financial officer, a leader for human resources, a chief operating officer, the leaders for each operating division, a chief technology officer and director of the Agilent Laboratories, a chief information officer, and a general counsel. Each step of the way, the officers he had selected helped him choose those who followed. He also created his "governance" team, a new board, which included individuals with a wide range of experiences who could bring fresh ideas to the start-up company.

Then the work began. Barnholt and his leadership team spent days and days together. The focus wasn't on becoming a team, per se. There wasn't time. They had to agree on the goals for the new company, their performance targets, their values, and the culture they wished to build. They also needed to divide critical responsibilities among themselves. Myriad details had to be resolved to start a new stand-alone $8 billion high-technology company, one of the largest Silicon Valley initial public offering to that time, and to disentangle their many connections with the HP parent. They also had to run the company—producing, distributing, and marketing their products and building their new brand. By solving real problems and consciously reflecting on their progress as they did so, they learned how to work with one another and what the rules for their team would be. Barnholt's role throughout was to provide a focal point for the team and inspiration for the venture. He was the only one who could make certain decisions, and as CEO he had to play roles no one else could. He led the discussions with Wall Street and the investment community, for example, met regularly with employees, and was the final arbiter for many crucial decisions. But even these apparently individual actions were taken only after collaboration, dialogue, and input from many sources and ongoing discussions with the senior leadership team and the board of directors. Team activities and the shared decisions occurred face-to-face and by phone conference, email, voice mail, and fax. Information was shared constantly and communication never stopped.

Barnholt and his senior leaders also created a small team of eight to ten people from across the organization to lead the integration of their financial, HR, and manufacturing-support software systems into a single, common system for the company. This isn't unusual. Many companies have already done this or are doing it now. It is difficult work, however. The Agilent leaders, like those of many other companies, used a team to carry out this difficult task. Their reasoning: To be successful, the integration required in-depth understanding of the company. No single individual had this knowledge, so several people needed to be involved. The team enabled them to share their knowledge and experience and to integrate and coordinate their work. Helping the project team were scores of additional teams focused on specific elements of the integration project.

One must search carefully to find work that isn't done by a team of one form or another in Agilent. So deeply ingrained in the culture is teamwork and collaboration that individuals who disrupt team performance because of their need for independence are denied promotions and even asked to leave the organization. There are exceptions, of course. Agilent requires strong individual contributors. But wherever you go in the company, collaboration and teamwork are basic values, and the team is the way those values are brought together to get work done. A healthy Agilent, Barnholt believes, depends on the insight that groups of individuals are best suited to accomplish; the challenges are almost always too complex to entrust to a single person.

### Example Two: The Major Consulting Companies

A consultant colleague of mine once observed that the "Renaissance Consultant doesn't exist." The complex problems that companies face are usually beyond the ability of a single person to understand or solve. The knowledge companies know this. Firms that have consulted with organizations I've been part of— Booz Allen Hamilton, Deloitte and Touche, McKinsey, Boston Consulting Group, A. T. Kearney, Delta, Price Waterhouse Coopers—use teams to carry out their work. So do legal and accounting firms, investment banks, and real-estate advisers. The consulting companies provide several important lessons for medicine.

Some consulting "teams" are nothing more than support groups of junior associates who do the heavy lifting for the senior partners. But carefully constructed and supported teams are the fundamental organizational unit of these firms, and, as in Agilent Technologies, teamwork and collaboration are their central values. Team performance drives their success, so much so that strong individual performers, even long-standing members of the firm, risk being terminated if they disrupt the work of teams. Considerable effort is devoted to making sure that teams have the appropriate mix of people to address the problem they've been asked to address. At the outset of each new assignment, team members agree on the rules: (1) what the role of each person will be, (2) how decisions will be made, (3) who has the final say on any given matter, and (4) how work will be divided among the team members. Every team has a leader, a final arbiter in the event decisions can't be reached together, someone who sets the agendas, maintains the calendars, and keeps things moving.

Except for the appointed team-leader role, successful teams are nonhierarchical; people check their status, titles, and organizational power at the door so that they can work together without that inhibition. When teams do not function well, internal experts help them get back on track. Members are replaced if they contribute to a team's problems. Individual team-member rewards are based on the performance of the team as a whole, and promotions in the competitive cultures at many of these firms are based on teamwork, team leadership, and contributions to the team, in addition to individual attributes. Teams are also used to introduce new recruits into the firms. Junior associates are assigned to teams and, through firsthand experience, learn the core values and practices of collaboration and teamwork.

## Observations

The experiences of Agilent Technologies and the large consulting firms prompt several observations that help us in medicine. The great value of teams is that they can address problems that no single individual can solve. The team provides a broader range of ideas and perspectives, leading to better solutions. The team can also help those involved in these complex matters to coordinate their work and respond to problems that arise in the course of implementing a project and its solutions. Without the team, work is more likely to be fragmented and more expensive. For the care of patients with chronic or complex conditions, the team offers significant promise, precisely because the care requirements are so challenging.

We can observe from the experience of Agilent and consulting firms that teams don't just happen. Teams work because of attention and resources, not wishful thinking. Several characteristics of successful teams can be identified. The right people must be selected and constant reinforcement provided to help the team get better at what it wishes to do. Clear rules must be established about leadership, team behavior, communications, decision-making, and resolving conflict among team members. A common understanding of the problem is essential, as is a shared agreement about solutions and implementation. Learning through team self-evaluation, analysis of team results, and individual and team-based exploration of new ideas is basic to building and maintaining team effectiveness. A successful team, then, is a highly disciplined collection of people brought together to perform tasks and functions that are too complex and critical for them to do alone or carry out independently of one another without serious consequences. Taking care of patients is always the priority among clinicians, as it should be. But time and resources for building and maintaining teams must come from somewhere. This inherent tension has to be addressed if medicine is to incorporate team solutions into daily patient-care practice.

Teams are not the solution to every medical problem or situation. They are not a panacea. Some problems are best addressed by an individual, or by a two- or three-person group that works together without forming as a team. Sometimes the work of bringing people together is more trouble than it is worth. The decision to build and maintain a team must be made after weighing the advantages and disadvantages of this solution against the alternatives. Only when the benefits for the patient are greater than the time, energy, and resources required to create and support the team would one want to proceed with this alternative.

## Managing Knowledge and Skills

### The Issue

As we have seen in earlier chapters, medical science and technologies, chronic illness, and social diversity have placed huge burdens on the medical professional that overwhelm even the smartest, most highly motivated individual. Yet the responsibility for staying current rests on the solitary shoulders of the individual professional. Fortunately, that professional has some help. Specialty societies, professional organizations and journals, websites, and tools such as handheld devices with drug formularies provide some assistance. But medicine lacks sophisticated systems to provide doctors and other medical professionals with what they need to care for us when we need it.

This means that you are likely to seek care from a physician who, like Dr. Landers described in earlier chapters, struggles to stay current with the rapid changes in medicine diagnosis and treatment. You don't know if your physician is using the tools that give you the best chance of getting better and avoiding complications. When you go to surgery, you don't know whether the surgeon's judgment and skills are strong enough to ensure the safest and most appropriate surgical outcome. Checks and balances like state-licensing boards, specialty certification systems, and hospital privileging systems provide some controls. But other industries do far more to help professionals manage the onslaught of information and discovery, as well as to assure that their knowledge, judgments, and skills are sufficiently advanced to protect those who depend on them.

### Example One: Supporting Knowledge and Skill Development in the Knowledge Companies

We turn again to the large global consulting companies. These firms sell solutions; their product is knowledge and judgment. With thousands of consultants of widely different backgrounds working in offices throughout the globe, the challenge of maintaining knowledge and skills is daunting. Yet these firms, run by the consultants themselves, keep track of who knows what and who can do what. The partners know who has dealt with what problems and where they can be reached. They keep detailed and easily accessed information on the problems they have encountered, the solutions chosen, and the evaluation of their impact. In addition, they track developments outside the firm that help them better serve their clients. The collective knowledge and skills of the firm are readily available at all times, day or night, across the globe.

The consultants, then, have developed sophisticated systems to help build and maintain knowledge and skills.

- *Accountability for managing and building the knowledge and skills support systems throughout the firm is assigned to a senior leader or designated leaders.* At Booz Allen Hamilton, a respected senior partner is the full-time "chief knowledge officer."

- *Information systems are the backbone of today's sophisticated knowledge support systems.* Booz Allen Hamilton consultants enter detailed information into the firm-wide knowledge database on each assignment: issues, problems, ideas, solutions, and results. Partners are expected to draw information from the common database at all stages of subsequent engagements.

- *Teams provide for knowledge sharing and skill building.* At McKinsey Company, care is given to constructing consultant teams with complementary skills and experiences who will work well together to foster creativity, collaboration, and learning.

- *Outside experts meet with internal consultants to share new ideas.* The best firms constantly seek new ideas and new approaches from outside the firm. Deloitte and Touche does this in regular meetings that bring together consultants from across the firm to meet with outside experts. Internal consultants are also encouraged to work with academics and researchers and to explore emerging concepts and approaches in order to remain at the forefront of thinking about the problems they face.

- *Regular evaluations during and after consulting engagements ensure that new ideas, important knowledge, and new skills are incorporated into the ongoing work.* Rigorous evaluation is an important tool for learning. The issues are real, immediate, and personal. At McKinsey, systematic evaluations conducted by nonteam partners during and after each major consulting effort are shared widely and incorporated into the firm's database.

- *Consultants are rigorously assessed on their knowledge and skills.* People work together on virtually every assignment. If someone isn't up to date, hasn't taken advantage of the data and archives, doesn't know what's going on in the field in which he is working, or has difficulty working collaboratively, the failings are soon obvious. There's no place to hide.

### Example Two: Ensuring That Skills Are Up-to-Date in the Airline Industry

The commercial airline industry ensures that its pilots are able to fly their passengers safely. To retain his right to fly, a commercial pilot must complete a prescribed number of hours of retraining each year and successfully pass a rigorous exam that assesses competence in normal and emergency situations. Flight simulators are used for these tests. The pilot who fails can fly only under direct supervision until he successfully passes the examinations. Less commonly, the pilot loses his license to fly. A body of law joins with a strong safety culture in commercial aviation to support this rigor and accountability.

## Observations

At some point, the complexity of issues overwhelms the ability of the individual to keep up. Successful firms have responded by recognizing the value of knowledge and skills to their ability to perform and by investing in the creation of robust systems to help. Typically, these systems require significant information-technology platforms, although a characteristic of all is the use of a combination of additional approaches. The challenges that medical professionals face are ones that greater individual effort alone will not enable them to manage. The dilemma is to find the resources and the organizational structures to build and maintain the systems that medicine now requires.

Keeping up is only part of the challenge. The best firms build decision-support tools into their knowledge-management systems so that individuals and teams have easy access to information they need. Applying this concept to medicine is particularly difficult. Physicians and other clinicians see a large number of patients each day, many with distinct problems. Thus far, medicine has struggled to make decision-support tools that are simple and accessible enough for use in daily practice. Incorporating changes in medical practice when they occur adds to the challenge. Until physicians or large collections of physicians agree on a decision-support solution, updates have to occur one doctor at a time.

Finally, the craft-based model of the autonomous professional in medicine places primary responsibility for maintaining knowledge, judgment, and skills with the individual professional or the institutions that the professionals create or choose. Accountability is inwardly directed rather than directed to the interest of the public. In the aviation industry, laws and culture added public-safety accountability to the airlines themselves when the strong professional culture of the pilots was deemed necessary but not sufficient to protect the passengers and the interests of the companies. In medicine, public and institutional accountability is limited. The legal accountabilities of health plans, hospitals, and other institutions for the skills of those who practice under their aegis have been expanded, albeit slowly, often with fierce resistance from physicians. For the most part, written testing and colleague assessments are the tools for assuring skills even within these institutions. Simulators, although used in a limited number of training programs, have not been employed to test judgment and skills, even though advanced computing, communications, and technology tools make this use possible. The issue is motivation and culture, not capacity.

## Quality, Cost, and Affordability

### The Issue

We often hear that each improvement in medical care—new drugs, new diagnostic capabilities, new surgeries, new monitoring techniques, new insurance benefits—increases rather than reduces costs and makes medical care less affordable. It is a mantra, and it leads to the unpalatable conclusion that the only way to stem the rising costs of medical care is to restrict care.

Many companies and organizations outside medicine have demonstrated that this common wisdom is wrong: They have reduced costs successfully by improving quality. They use sophisticated tools to identify any flaws in design, organization, and production and to determine how to make changes in these areas to deliver products and services that meet quality specifications. The winners of the nation's highest award for quality, the Baldridge Award, routinely demonstrate significant improvements, often in the range of 25 to 30 percent according to Robert Galvin, former Chairman and CEO of Motorola, and a founder of the Baldridge Award, in their underlying cost structures as a result of their quality-improvement efforts.

When outsiders view the chaos in medical care, the redundancies and errors, the fragmentation and confusion, the miscommunications when care is delivered to seriously ill patients, and the wide variation in the way physicians practice, they cannot accept that higher quality should cost more. Their experience suggests the opposite, and their logic is compelling. If well-organized manufacturing and service organizations can achieve significant savings by improving quality, then even greater opportunity exists in medicine. Estimates of the cost of poor quality in medicine support their argument. Poor quality—overuse, misuse, underuse, errors, lost information, repeat procedures, failed communications, poor design of care processes, wide differences in the way doctors practice in spite of medical science, and the like—may consume as much as 30 to 40 cents of every dollar spent for medical care. Poor quality, not higher quality, is a major contributor to the growing cost of medical care.*

Consider the hernia operation. A patient sees his primary-care physician, confirms that the unpleasant-looking lump in the groin is a hernia, and schedules surgery. Prior to the operation, the patient goes in for preoperative lab tests, possibly a chest X ray, depending on the hospital, sees the anesthesiologist and returns twenty-four hours later for surgery. The patient checks into the waiting area, gets the preanesthesia drugs, and then is taken to the operating room, where the anesthesiologist administers the local or general anesthetic and the surgeon performs the operation, aided by a nurse or physician assistant. After surgery, the patient spends a few hours in the recovery room, is examined once again by the surgeon, sees the anesthesiologist, and is discharged to go home. A week or two later, the patient is checked once again by the surgeon to make sure the scar is healing and the surgery was successful. That's it. The patient interacts with three doctors and several nurses. Simple. Hardly.

---

*Of course, other factors contribute, too: aging, chronic illness, legal protection, and advances in medical science, for example. But poor quality remains a major driver, if not the major contributor, to the overall costs of care.

For this uncomplicated and routine operation, the patient interacted with at least eight to ten different medical professionals in six different settings. Information had to move from one professional to another and one site to another, and the right data had to be linked to the right patient. Lab work and X rays had to be ordered, performed properly, and interpreted correctly (by another set of professionals), and the results had to be provided to the surgeon and anesthesiologist in time for the operation. Supplies such as gloves and operating equipment had to be available in the right form, with everything working properly when needed. Administrative tasks had to be coordinated so that the patient and the family could move from place to place without delays or inconvenience. Behind the three doctors and the many nurses were individuals whose work had to be designed and executed flawlessly to complement those taking direct care of the patient. Just think about the person who moved the patient from one place to the next; the ones who did the paperwork or the lab work; or those who took and developed the X rays. Think about the people who made sure the equipment was cleaned properly and taken to the right operating room for the surgeon; or those who cleaned the operating room after it was used. Still more were involved behind the scenes in the recovery room and the discharge area. You get the idea. Even something as apparently simple as a hernia operation is a complex process. It certainly isn't done by one person with a scalpel.

Imagine how hard this is to get right when every primary-care doctor and surgeon and anesthesiologist does things his way. Think about how many different pieces of equipment, processes, operating approaches, recovery procedures, and discharge decisions have to be made to support this independence. Imagine what it's like for the hospital staff. Imagine what it does to costs. Then think about what happens when each step is organized to be independent of the next. Think about what this does to the chances that information won't get from one place to the next, or that laboratory results will get put in the wrong chart, or that critical conversations at each step of the way won't get passed along. Or that misunderstandings will occur that result in the wrong medicine being given, or the wrong side being operated on.

As long as medicine is made up of independent, autonomous craftsmen, each making his own judgments based on his interpretation of the science he remembers, and relying on skills that may or may not be up to date, the opportunities to improve quality cannot apply. Quality in traditional medicine has been a measure of individual competence—how well the doctor takes care of each patient. This is quite important, a necessary component in addressing the opportunities in medicine. But it is far from sufficient, offering only modest gains in quality and reductions in costs. The great opportunities for improving our care and lowering the costs to produce it lie with the way care is knit together for us.

We see this potential in examples drawn from other industries that highlight four related approaches to quality improvement and cost management. The first involves the use of sophisticated analytic and design tools to reengineer the entire production process for the Boeing 777 aircraft, arguably one of the most complex and demanding production processes in manufacturing today. A similar process is described at an Agilent Technologies manufacturing plant in Singapore. The third example involves the use of mass-production techniques to improve quality and reduce costs at USAA, a large insurance company. By distinguishing activities that are repetitive and standard from those that must be tailored to the individual consumer, USAA has maintained a competitive array of choices, industry-leading service, high customer loyalty, and highly competitive prices. The final example is General Electric Company, which has achieved product-reliability levels that are among the highest in the industry—3 deficiencies for every 1 million products or services produced—reducing operating costs and improving profitability as a result.

## Example One: Boeing Company and the Redesign of the 777

Along with Airbus in Europe, Boeing manufactures the majority of the world's commercial jet aircraft fleet. The Boeing 777 is one of the most advanced. Building it is extremely complex, and the demands for quality cannot be compromised. As with errors in medicine, when jets fail, the results are catastrophic.

After designing and producing the first series of 777s, a safer, more fuel-efficient plane than Airbus offered, Boeing managers realized that they couldn't compete because Boeing's costs were too high and its production time too long. So the managers and systems engineers set out to redesign the entire production process to produce an airplane that retained its superior performance characteristics and was less expensive to manufacture. Further, they wanted to reduce the time from order to completion, as every day saved meant that Boeing would be paid earlier and purchasers would be able to put the plane into service sooner.

The managers and engineers were faced with a massive challenge. The 777 contains more than 87.8 miles of wiring, 27.2 miles of tubes, and 3.2 million separate parts from more than 545 suppliers. A total of 9,294 distinct steps occur in the production process, involving 6,000 people working in six major Boeing sites where different parts are built up into subassemblies. The redesign teams worked for a year to lay out the entire production process, step by step, part by part, person by person. They identified how to reduce unnecessary steps, how to improve the design of parts to make them easier to attach, and how to tighten the quality requirements to superior tolerance levels to reduce the number of parts that had to be discarded. They redesigned specific clusters of steps to manufacture different components—a wing assembly, or a landing gear, for example—in order to simplify the process and limit the production errors that caused delays. They renegotiated their agreements with suppliers. They retrained people, redefined jobs, and automated steps wherever possible to increase production speed and reliability. They added new production-tracking information technologies to give them minute details about production performance and to ensure that critical information passed from one step to the next.

As a result of their efforts, the number of steps in the process was reduced from 9,294 to 7,621, an 18 percent drop. The number of parts was reduced by 15 percent, and the number of suppliers from 545 to 380. These changes produced important results for the company. The total number of days required to produce a new 777 was reduced 30 percent, bringing higher revenue per plane and lower carrying costs. The profit margins on the plane rose significantly and the number of sale closures against the Airbus improved considerably. CEO Phil Condit believes that the redesign was a key factor in improving annual profits, starting in 1998.

### Example Two: Agilent Technologies in Singapore

The same attention to production design and performance can be seen at the manufacturing plants run by Agilent Technologies. Once the laboratories have designed a new product and engineers have learned to produce it, the manufacturing process is moved to Singapore. Part of the reason is that wages are lower, though not appreciably. The real advantage to production in Singapore is the superior design and operations talent. Agilent puts much of its high-tech manufacturing in Singapore because the professionals there are so good at it.

At one plant I visited, complex optical switches, tiny in size, were produced in sparkling clean rooms by workers in space-age suits, goggles, and hats using electron microscopes and highly advanced machinery and information technologies. What caught my attention when I toured the plant were printed graphs attached to one of the floor-to-ceiling windows that separated the production area from the observation stations. The graph showed defects per 1 million switches on the y-axis and time in weeks on the $x$-axis. In the first twelve weeks of production, the line on the graph started at a relatively high level of defects but fell steadily with each week until a steady state of around 3 defects per 1 million switches was reached. Another graph displayed the cost to produce each unit; it, too, showed a steady decline corresponding to the improvement in quality. When I complemented the production supervisor on this performance, he looked puzzled. I explained that I was impressed with the rapid improvement in quality and the corresponding reduction in manufacturing costs. He shrugged his shoulders impatiently. "There's no magic in this," he told me. "We study every step and make the necessary adjustments until we get it right. Then we keep working to make it better. What you see now is our baseline target performance. Come back in a year and it will be even better." Then he paused, still bemused by my question. "This is what we do every day," he concluded. "It's our work."

## Example Three: USAA

I joined the U.S. Armed Forces Association's insurance and financial services organization (USAA) in 1967 as a public health services physician and have purchased car and home insurance from it ever since. The association, with $60 billion in assets and customers located around the world, is highly regarded for its competitive prices, outstanding service, and responsive, innovative products.

USAA performs well because of its extensive use of mass-customization tools. It uses sophisticated information systems to provide agents with ready-made and up-to-date information, premium quotes, and the ability to mix and match products as required by the customer. In their database is information about local agents and shops used for insurance estimates and car repairs. Agents receive extensive training: The target is to resolve 95 percent of all phone calls without transfer to another part of the organization or a higher official. Each time I've needed an automobile repaired after a collision (we have four children, now young adults; as a result, we know USAA quite well!), agents have made referrals quickly and maintained regular communications until repairs are completed. Claims are paid promptly, disputes are handled expeditiously, and regular satisfaction surveys give me the opportunity to provide feedback.

USAA has carefully analyzed its business to determine routine customer needs: information requests, descriptions of product options, quotes, claims, and referrals. All is standardized and supported by information systems in order to avoid placing the burden of figuring out what to do for these routine matters on the agents themselves. The agents, in turn, collect information using standardized questionnaires. They concentrate on understanding what the customer is looking for and what the particular requirements are. These customer requirements are then matched to standardized charts and products; the result is a form of mass customization. If the agents were not supported in this way, they would have to design each product from the ground up, as if they were doing it for the first and only time for that customer.

When I call, they have my insurance history in front of them, as well as information about my family and me. Again, using information technology, they can match this information with products that I might be interested in, a form of mass customization, and suggest alternatives to me either over the phone or by mail. Because I trust the company and have worked with it for thirty-plus years, I don't view this as intrusive. Quite the contrary. I am grateful that the agents make the suggestions because I know that their products are reliable. And, of course, I can always say no.

USAA is rated as one of the 100 best companies in the United States to work for. Its agents are highly ethical and very responsive. Never have I had reason to question their ability to protect the privacy of the information they have about my family. They enjoy lifelong relationships with a large and growing number of highly satisfied, loyal customers who, like me, wouldn't consider going anywhere else to meet their needs.

## Example Four: GE and Six Sigma Quality

Led by then Chairman and CEO Jack Welch, in 1995 the General Electric Company launched an aggressive campaign to reduce operating costs by making significant improvements in quality. Drawing on the experiences of major companies like Motorola, Allied Signal/Honeywell, and others, the GE leadership team challenged their company to take $5 billion out of its operating costs by reducing the number of defects in the goods it manufactures and the services it provides. Their goal was to have the entire company operating at a rate of 3.4 defects for every 1 million products produced. As defined in the quality literature, this is called a "Six Sigma Quality" level of performance, a level achieved only by companies with highly aggressive and focused quality-management programs.

The GE Six Sigma campaign has focused on designing more reliable products and more consistent production processes. If it took five days to close the books at the end of the month, the leaders asked the financial teams to figure out how to close them in two or to achieve performance that matched the best in the world, both in terms of speed and accuracy. If 5 jet engines failed out of every 1 million installed on jet aircraft, the designers and manufacturing plants were challenged to figure out how to reduce the number of defects to 3.4 per 1 million. Simply stated, the GE Six Sigma program has concentrated on getting things right so that products and services come as close to never failing as humanly possible. No corner of the company has been left untouched. Efforts were made to measure everything possible in terms of time required, errors and failures, costs, customer complaints, and inventories. You name it, and GE probably measured it to see how much it varied from day to day and how often it failed to meet the acceptable range of performance.

To carry out the campaign, GE used:

- Consistent leadership support.

- Extensive training throughout the entire company in the techniques of Six Sigma and the goals and expectations of the company leaders.

- Highly trained operating leaders for the Six Sigma teams and efforts.

- Strong accountability for results.

- Incentives and rewards to reinforce the work.

- Regular and systematic reporting of improvements and accomplishments.

- Financial tracking to assure that the program achieves the desired financial goals.

The focus on quality improvement has paid large dividends for GE. GE goods and services are considered the best in their class. In most instances, their defect rates are among the lowest anywhere. This achievement is reassuring for those of us who fly on airplanes that use GE jet engines, get our electricity from companies that use GE turbines, or have studies and procedures performed on us using GE medical equipment. The other benefit is financial: an estimated $750 million in savings in 1998, a forecasted $1.5 billion by 1999, and expectations of several more billions down the road. In the first several years of the campaign, GE regularly hit new records quarter after quarter for operating margins and profitability, results that GE leaders attribute in significant part to the Six Sigma efforts.

## Observations

These tools cannot be applied to medicine without significant modifications. Medicine, after all, is not a product that doctors and medical professionals make. Taking care of patients involves much more than answering questions over the phone and delivering insurance products, or building fail-safe products. We're talking about people who rely on doctors and medical professionals for their care and their comfort; about medical science that is far from perfect or precise in spite of the advances over the years.

This said, the tools to improve quality and affordability and reduce costs have major potential for medicine. Return to the hernia operation. Think of what it would mean if the risk of something going wrong decreased tenfold. Or think about how important it is to get the right medications to reduce pain, decrease nausea, and shorten one's stay in the recovery room. Or that everyone gets a call the morning after surgery to make sure there are no complications. Or that there are no delays in surgery because paperwork is incomplete or hasn't arrived on time. Think of what it means to pay one-third less for an operation that is done right, without errors, and gives the best chance of recovering rapidly and without complications. Or if fewer medicines were required but they relieved symptoms more effectively. The tools described above, properly adapted to medicine, offer this potential.

Let's be more specific. If 90 percent of patients getting a hernia repair have the same laboratory tests, why not have patients go directly to the lab at the preanesthesia workup? If 90 percent of the patients receive the same preanesthesia medications, why not have them prepackaged on the floor in ready-to-use containers? Similarly, if all of the patients are having a hernia repair, why not get the surgeons to agree on a standard equipment pack for the operating room and standard orders for recovery? Both can be customized as required by the individual patient, just as medications can and must be adjusted. But by planning for the usual and making sure the usual is done as close to perfectly as possible for every patient, the physicians and medical professionals can concentrate on the exceptions and the judgments and skills required to perform flawlessly. By laying out the entire care process, from preanesthesia visit to discharge, one can discover where work gets repeated unnecessarily, where stays are prolonged, and where errors occur. One can see how to reduce steps and improve consistency through better routines and training, as well as through better design of the steps along the way. And by constantly analyzing performance for each part of the process, measuring how often tasks are performed at the desired level, one can identify opportunities to improve.

Now apply the same reasoning to someone with a lifelong disease, such as diabetes or asthma, for example. Multiply the people, steps, places, equipment, medications, procedures, and tests by many hundreds of times beyond the requirements for a hernia repair. The tools are essential for fitting together the pieces of something as complex as chronic-illness care, for delivering care to each of us that is as close to flawless as science allows. These tools are well developed in other industries, basic to running superior manufacturing and services companies around the world. It is their work.

A final word about the relationship between quality and cost. The total costs of medical care may not actually go down as a result of these efforts. Medical care continues to expand: More care is available for a wider array of conditions because of breakthroughs in medical science and new technologies. This progress drives costs up. So do a host of other factors unrelated to the design and performance of the delivery system itself. If history is a guide, these costs are likely to accelerate faster than the underlying performance of the professionals and the care systems can be improved and costs reduced. The tools described, applied rigorously to medical care, will improve quality and help build the delivery-system infrastructure into which the new science and technologies can fit. In so doing, they can significantly moderate the rate of growth in costs over time. Whether or not the improvements can overcome the upward cost pressures on medicine remains to be seen.

# Organization

## The Issue

What is it about organizations? Doctors hate the idea. Patients distrust them. And there aren't very many of them around. To many, organizations mean bureaucracy, rigidity, impersonality, lockstep conformity, and indifference to the needs of the people in them or those served by them. If organizations are bad, big organizations are worse. The organizations in medicine are, for the most part, collections of hospitals, nursing homes, laboratories, or free-standing surgical centers—pieces of the puzzle that focus on one particular element of medical care.

Few organizations integrate the professionals and the institutions of medicine to streamline care for the patient. In fact, researcher Stephen Shortell and his colleagues have reported that the number of integrated delivery systems has remained unchanged over the past decade and that efforts to integrate care within those that exist have been reduced in the face of other, more immediate competitive concerns. Certainly, organizations like Group Health Cooperative of Puget Sound, HealthPartners, Kaiser Permanente, the Harvard Pilgrim system, and several others continue to push for greater care integration. But these are the exceptions.

The organization plays a critical role in medical-care delivery, as we will see in the next chapter. So our challenge is to find ways to create organizations in medicine that support better patient care while responding to the concerns that patients and providers alike have about them. Stated differently, we have to design organizations so that dislike and distrust are replaced by confidence and appreciation. Only this way will organizations grow in number and be able to support the delivery of medical care for the better.

Again, we can draw lessons from the experiences of others.

### Example One: Birds and Boats

Paul Plesac, an organizational theorist who works with Don Berwick at the Institute for Healthcare Improvement, offers a delightful insight. Flocks of birds never collide in flight. They swoop, glide, rise, and alight together without running into one another. They chatter a lot once they perch, but while they're flying, they are often surprisingly silent. They don't need committees or meetings to decide what to do. Nor do they take orders from a leader. Instead, they operate with a few basic rules: stay close to the birds on either side; stay with the flock; and fly well. Using these simple rules, it is possible to model the behavior of the birds on a computer. The flocks are self-organizing: Apply these simple rules, and they stay together and fly together.

We can learn from the birds in the design of organizations capable of responding to continuously changing situations. Like the Navy. When you think of the Navy, you think of chains of command, rules, uniforms, and standard operating procedures. And for normal circumstances, this system works pretty well. But when a huge destroyer or aircraft carrier is under attack, there's no time to send information up the chain of command. To deal with this, the Navy has adopted a form of self-organization like the birds. Personnel have been trained extensively, a few clear limits are set, and the personnel at all levels are turned loose to "fly well." The chain of command is superseded by small groups or teams working on one part of the response—guns, missiles, evasion, and the like.

### Example Two: Pizza and Potential

Pizza has been the brain-food for endless brainstorming sessions and work groups in the United States. Easy, fast, informal, it encourages conversation (between bites) and supports the exciting spontaneous combustion that characterizes high-performing organizations. Pizza is a metaphor for the more informal, less hierarchical, more creative and responsive organization that many leaders have tried to create. A number of high-tech firms sprinkled around the Bay Area, especially in Silicon Valley, are renowned for their experiments in organizational design and culture. GE introduced a highly interactive group problem-identification and problem-solving process called "workouts." These organizations are designed to encourage debate and openness, experimentation and learning, all of which demand informality and eliminate invasive hierarchy. They are designed to respond quickly, to try new things, to move within broad boundaries of values and performance expectations, and to operate with only a short list of dos and don'ts.

## Sharing Leadership

Companies as diverse as Caterpillar, Harley Davidson, and Northwest Natural Gas, among many others, have engaged their workforces in critical decisions about their companies. Typically, but not always, these are unionized companies; the unions have forged partnerships with management to drive the performance and make strategic decisions for the company. This is a far different approach from the traditional separation and tension that have characterized labor-management relationships for decades. The core ideas are that labor and management share a stake in the future of the company, and that the perspectives of both are required to address the challenges the company faces in today's world and to apply the tools required to constantly improve performance.

We've done this at Kaiser Permanente. Together with the AFL-CIO, we have created a partnership that involves twenty-five of our thirty-six unions, thirty-five of fifty-four separate labor agreements, and 60,000 of the 64,000 represented workers in the organization. All union affiliates in the partnership are part of AFL-CIO. One affiliate union chose not to participate; the remaining nonparticipants are not part of the AFL-CIO. A senior union official and a senior officer of Kaiser Permanente lead the partnership, together chairing a national steering committee of member union leaders and managers. The partnership is formalized in a cascading series of partnership teams and committees throughout the organization, where the day-to-day problem solving and agenda setting occurs. The process isn't easy; there are new behaviors to learn and old habits to break. But it is a far sight better than the contentious, divisive approach that Kaiser Permanente experienced in the past.

Another approach to shared leadership is found in the nation's cooperative movement. The largest cooperatives are in the farming and financial services industries, although several examples exist in medical care as well, notably Group Health Cooperative and HealthPartners in Minneapolis. These kinds of organizations have demonstrated, both in this country and in Europe, that those whom the organization serves can manage the affairs of the enterprise and compete successfully with other, more traditional organizational models.

Professional firms are another example of self-managing organizations. These include such things as accountancy companies, law firms, consultant firms, engineering firms, medical groups, and the like, which belie the canard that a "professional organization" is an oxymoron. They aren't easy to organize or manage; after all, they are made up of professionals who are socialized to function independently. Some fail to perform as expected. But they govern themselves, elect their own leaders, create their own boards, determine how they will be paid, establish their standards and requirements for performance, hold one another accountable, and grow the firm—all the things other companies and organizations seek to do.

## Observations

The demand for flexibility, responsiveness, speed, voice, and independence is not unique to medicine. Leaders and organizational design theorists have sought this Holy Grail in a variety of manufacturing, service, and professional organizations. Finding solutions may be more difficult in medicine because of the unique perspectives of the physicians and the intimacy required in the patient-clinician relationship. Certainly, there is no place in medicine for the rigid hierarchy, impersonal relationships, or lockstep conformity that characterize organizations at their worst. We can see in the examples just cited that an organization need not be antithetical to good care and caring, however. Rather, when attention is given to appropriate design and function, the organization becomes a critical element of the care process, one that cannot be provided in any other form.

# 7

# PUTTING IT TOGETHER

How do we incorporate Rebecca's experiences, the innovations in medical care, and the lessons from outside medicine into a delivery system for the twenty-first century that can meet the daunting challenges medicine confronts? We start with what we, as patients, want from our care. We want doctors and medical professionals to give us care that makes us better or helps control the pain and complications when we are sick. We want our care to be safe; we want our lives to be protected from errors committed by the people and institutions we ask to help us. We want to be treated as individuals who are shaped by our families, our culture, and our own capabilities. We want medical care to respond to our need for comfort, to our fears, and to our uncertainties. And we want it to be within our reach financially.

To achieve these goals in the world medicine faces today, we need care that:

- Addresses our individual requirements for independence, information, and access.

- Ensures that those who care for us are up to date and safely use the right medical science and technology to treat us.

- Organizes to treat our illnesses.

- Manages the complex business, legal and regulatory, and accountability requirements of medicine as well as possible.

- Addresses the medical conditions and expectations that are part of our different backgrounds: racial, ethnic, religious, cultural, and linguistic.

- Helps us when bioterrorism, imported disease, or environmental toxins threaten us.

For most of us, the personal relationship we have with our physician is the most critical requirement we have. It is here that the trust is established that is so essential to getting better and being comforted when we are sick or worried. As we move from simple illnesses and minor injuries to more complex ones, the importance of that relationship grows. For routine problems we want to be treated as conveniently as we can. We don't require a lot of time. But when we journey further into the unknown, or when our lives are threatened or the quality of our lives is disrupted, our needs for comfort and reassurance grow, and the importance of the personal relationship grows with them.

How, then, can we fit these requirements into a coherent picture? The starting place is the *care team*, where we join with our physician and other medical professionals to get most of the care we need. The *organization* provides support to enable us to receive the best possible care and move safely and easily from one part of the care system to another as we are diagnosed and treated. This is the second piece of the puzzle. The third is the collection of resources within the *community* that help us learn about and manage our conditions. When care teams, organizations, and communities are joined effectively, the result is an *integrated, care team–based delivery system*. Although we cannot yet define how each element will operate in the future or exactly how the pieces will fit together, we can explore core functions that will drive them forward in their evolution. We want innovation to continue to keep pace with the rapid changes both within medicine and from the environment in which it resides.

## The Care Team

The care team is the fundamental building block of our care. It is here that our doctor and a handful of medical professionals work together day after day to meet our needs. This is where the human relationships at the heart of medicine occur, where we establish the trust we seek, and where we receive the support we want and need. It is here that we learn to manage our medications and our rehabilitation, to maintain our health, and to recognize and prevent complications. It is where we question, and where we discover how to adapt care to our needs. We venture out from the safe harbor of our care team when we need the help of additional doctors and medical professionals or need care in hospitals, nursing homes, or the other institutions of medicine.

### Members

As patients, we are at the center of the care team, our own primary caregivers. Around us are a small number of professionals, between three and eight, depending on the conditions and needs we have.

- *Our Doctor:* Our doctor is a critical member of the team, often leading it, and bringing knowledge, skills, and experience that are crucial to us as patients. Our doctor diagnoses the specific illness, anticipates and recognizes medical complications when they occur, and matches specific medications and other treatments (such as surgery) to the condition as it evolves over time. Often, our physician is the person we rely on to help us make decisions about our care and to make sense of the information and recommendations we get from others.

- *Nurse Care Manager:* This highly trained professional, often the glue for the team, has the most regular contact with us and our families and helps coordinate and integrate the care that occurs both inside the team and outside of it from other teams and individual professionals. The nurse is the traffic controller, dispatcher, navigator, and often the adviser, counselor, and comforter as well.

- *Other Physicians:* In addition to the primary physician, other specialists may become members of the team, depending on the situation. The person with diabetes may require care from a cardiologist, a nephrologist, an ophthalmologist, an endocrinologist, and even a surgeon.

- *Other Professionals:* Nutritionists are often valuable when dealing with heart disease, diabetes, or renal disease. Pharmacists provide valuable insights into the management and tracking of complex or powerful medications. Social workers help link patients and families with community-support sources. Health educators bring special skills in patient education. Nurse practitioners and physician assistants are highly trained clinicians who can extend the capabilities of the physician.

## Form

Teams will take many forms. A primary-care team may bring together physicians, nurse practitioners, physician assistants, and other caregivers to work with patients and families with a wide range of conditions, from simple and self-limited to complex and chronic ones. Special focus teams may deal with specific conditions, illnesses, or interventions: renal dialysis, diabetes, cancers, asthma, surgeries, intensive care, and many more. Teams may specialize in prevention and screening for colorectal cancer, breast cancer, prostate cancer, or immunizations. They may deal with health maintenance in the elderly, in healthy adults, or in the young, addressing issues of diet, exercise, stress, smoking cessation, and other lifestyle-related matters.

## Purpose

Whatever the makeup and the form of the team, its central purpose is to provide us with the relationships and skills we need to manage our conditions. The team is also designed to provide us with consistent and coordinated care, based on the best that medical science can give us.

## Requirements

- *Team Building:* Teams cannot and will not spring into existence simply because we want them to; they don't develop into highly functioning units without work. They require practice, skill building, and a self-conscious effort to improve. Team members must learn to make decisions together, talk with one another, share information, and discuss the choices, treatments, and results. They must have time to think about what they are doing and what they have done, to reflect and consider alternatives together. Team members must learn to draw on one another for ideas and help. All of this takes time, both in the early stages and throughout the care

process. As much energy must be devoted to helping the team function at its highest possible level as
is given to maintaining the capabilities and skills of
the individuals who are members of the team. Fa-
cilitators or troubleshooters may be required to
move the team forward at certain times in its development.

• *Team Function:* A high-performing team requires explicit agreements among its members in several crucial areas. First, the team must agree on who its
leader is. Then the members must decide how they
will work together, make decisions, and manage dis-
agreements. They must agree on their purpose and
the values to guide them as they seek to achieve this
purpose. They have to establish clear guidelines
about how they will care for the patients they serve
and how to share information with one another.
Agreements must be reached about when the patient
and the team will meet, when the rest of the team will
meet without the patient, and how the information
that emerges from these interactions will be shared.

• *Team Support:* To work well as a team requires systems to support communications among the members
of the team, and in particular between the patient and
the doctor and between the patient and the other
team members. The system must include whatever
works to help patients get what they need: face-to-
face communications, written or faxed memos and
documents, telephone contact, voice mail or email
messages, and clinical databases. Information systems
are essential to store and move clinical information
among the team members and from one team to another. These systems are also required to capture and

share the knowledge that emerges from medical science and new technologies and from the experiences of the team itself. And they must be in place to provide for the data collection that is the basis for learning and improvement within the team. The team members must have access to new technologies and emerging medical science and the support required to analyze the information and new approaches and incorporate them into ongoing practice.

In the team-based model, it is rare that a physician, medical professional, or specialist acts as an independent craftsman—helped by a support staff, but acting on his own. Individual players may be able to care for simple, relatively straightforward illnesses. Or they may be specialists with highly focused expertise that care teams draw on. But even here, the demands of twenty-first-century medical care require many of the same tools that care teams need: communications, information, and knowledge-management systems, data, and the ability to interact effectively with other physicians and medical professionals. Without them, these throwbacks to the craft-based model will have difficulty participating within the larger medical community and will contribute to fragmentation and confusion just as the rest of medical care is beginning to find ways to bring care together for us.

## Organization

The care team needs organizational support. If each team designs its own solutions, we will have moved from the individual craftsman to the individual care-team with only a slight reduction in fragmentation and more confusion and lack of continuity. Doing things this way, team by team, adds significant cost and compromises our goal of affordability. Not only is it ill-advised for the individual care-team to take on the task of building its support capabilities, but the team lacks the perspectives, skills, and resources to do so. Moreover, it is not in a position to establish effective linkages to other teams and sources of support in the community. The organization does these things for the team.

## Members

A medical-care organization includes the individual professionals, the care teams, the support systems, the medical facilities and technologies, and the management to knit these elements together.

## Form

I suspect there are likely to be as many different kinds of organizations as there are people who wish to experiment with organizational design. They will be small or large. They will be not-for-profit, community-benefit organizations, cooperatives, or for-profit companies. Ideally they will be governed in a manner that ensures that we as patients, together with the professional caregivers, have a major voice in how care is delivered, how it is supported, and how well it is performing.

## Purpose

The purposes of the organization are threefold:

- To provide the scale required to generate the economic and intellectual resources that knit the various pieces of the medical-care puzzle into a coherent, integrated whole that works for us as patients.

- To assure accountability for the performance of the medical-care system it has brought together.

- To build the bridges with the community that make critical nonmedical resources available to us and to the medical professionals on whom we depend.

## Functions

The organization performs a host of vital tasks. It provides:

- Support services and linkages within the care team, among the teams, among the various players in medical-care delivery, whether or not they are part of teams (for example, hospital, hospice), and between the medical-care delivery system and the community.

- Communications and information-management infrastructure, including the knowledge-management systems to support professional growth and skill development.

- Coordination of patient-care requirements that enable patients to move from care team to care team without breaks in continuity, lost information, or conflicting diagnoses or treatments.

- Capital and human resources to build and maintain the support services divided among the care teams and other elements of the integrated system.

- Expertise, the intellectual firepower to help care teams to function, team members to work with one another, and teams to work together and to ensure that continuous improvement occurs.

- Expertise to knit the care processes together for our benefit when care extends beyond a single team.

- Data on performance to identify where care is working well and not so well, where errors are occurring, and the like.

- Assessments of how well the pieces of the puzzle fit together for patients as they move across the medical-care system.

- Accountability for overall performance: compliance with the best medical care that medical science and technologies can offer; safety; responsiveness to patients' needs and expectations; affordability; and ability to meet the diverse needs of patients.

- Resources to experiment with new organizational solutions that better serve patients' needs as medical-care changes.

- A buffer between the individual professionals and the outside world: the complex business environment, the insurers, and the legal and regulatory demands.

- A host of back-office administrative functions, such as accounting and finance, purchasing, human resources, facilities design and construction, and cash management, that the individual professional or care team would otherwise have to do themselves.

## Requirements

To be effective, organizations must:

- Ensure that we, as patients, as well as our caregivers have a major voice in the decisions that are made about how care is organized to serve us.

- Operate with clear and public expectations about and measurements of performance in terms of care effectiveness and safety, responsiveness, timeliness, costs and affordability, and ability to respond to social diversity.

- Support continuous education and development for us, our caregivers, and our care teams.

- Be flexible and responsive and willing to experiment with new organizational solutions and new relationships with the community.

- Be designed to minimize hierarchy and bureaucracy and to support the central role that the care teams play in delivering our care.

## Community

Without strong bridges to community expertise and resources, as we have seen, the care and support we receive may not give us the help we need. This is the third piece of the puzzle.

### Elements

The most important resources in the community are: the public health system; the advocacy organizations for specific diseases, patients, and population groups; and the alternative providers. In addition, depending on our specific problems, the resources may need to be expanded to include transportation, food, housing, environment, jobs, welfare, and community and faith-based organizations, as we saw with Claire Holland in Boston in chapter 5. In addition, there must be a bridge to the workplace to make sure that when we suffer from an illness or condition, our jobs are adjusted appropriately.

## The Public Health System

The public health system is chronically underfunded and often forgotten until a crisis like the anthrax outbreak of 2001 occurs. In truth, it is a linchpin in the care of those with complex or chronic conditions, in prevention and health-maintenance services, and in protecting us from the threats of bioterrorism, from infections brought into the United States from outside the country, and from environmental hazards. The public health system and the traditional medical-care system grew apart during the twentieth century and today operate in different worlds. We continue this separation at our peril because the public health system is critical in:

- Tracking illnesses in the community to determine when isolated incidents become epidemics and require major public and private interventions.

- Assessing how best to use disease screening and prevention tools.

- Identifying sources of infectious or environmental illnesses.

- Containing the spread and minimizing the public risks associated with infectious or environmental hazards through prevention, containment, clinical treatment, and public education.

- Assessing the health status of communities.

- Maintaining public health laboratories, vaccine storage facilities, and public health education capabilities.

Frequently complex to diagnose and treat, epidemic infectious and environmental illnesses can jeopardize fragile patients with chronic or complex conditions. Winter influenza outbreaks, for example, are dangerous for frail, elderly patients, for people with chronic lung and heart conditions, and for vulnerable young people. The public health system serves as the eyes and ears of the public and provides a source of critical expertise in the diagnosis, management, and monitoring of complex and chronic illness.

## Advocacy Groups

Consumer advocacy groups such as AARP for seniors, the National Partnership for Women & Families, Families USA, the Consumers Union, and a host of others can be a source of support and general medical information for medical consumers. Disease-specific organizations such as the American Heart Association, the American Cancer Society, the American Lung Association, the American Diabetes Association, and several others play a major role in helping patients find information that is helpful in understanding and obtaining treatment for our conditions.

These organizations:

- Provide educational materials and skill-building assistance to patients and their families.

- Connect patients with others concerned about the same problems.

- Identify providers in the community with special expertise, skills, and interest in serving patients and families with these conditions.

- Advocate for and support state and federal legislation to enhance research and care for specific groups or medical conditions.

- Frame legislation for health benefits, making sure that appropriate resources are devoted to care and ensuring that patients have explicit protections when their voices aren't heard or their care has been unsuccessful.

Knowledgeable advocates, often with more specialized information than many medical professionals have, can become valuable members of the care team for a patient or a group of patients with a common condition. They can also provide important help to the medical organizations that assume responsibility for organizing and supporting the care teams and for integrating care for the patients.

## Alternative Providers

Alternative providers—acupuncturists, chiropractors, yoga and meditation specialists, herbalists, and naturopaths—have joined care teams at the request of either the patient or other medical professionals.

Specifically:

- Chiropractors work on medical teams to help people with chronic back pain or joint disorders and to help with pre- and postsurgical rehabilitation for spinal disorders.

- Osteopathic physicians with special expertise in joint mobilization and skeletal manipulation have been included on orthopedic teams, in addition to providing primary care for patients in their traditional physician roles.

- Yoga and acupuncture specialists have participated in stress management, chronic-pain management, sports-injury management, and addiction management.

# Does It Work?

Experience with teams in caring for complex and chronic diseases and in carrying out prevention and health-maintenance activities is very encouraging. Patients who participate in care teams receive better care and have better results than patients who receive care in the traditional way. Part of the benefit comes from the patients themselves, who in the team-based model make decisions with their professional caregivers and learn to manage many day-to-day decisions about their conditions. Care given this way is less expensive, and, depending on who is on the care team, can address the needs of a wider cross section of our society more effectively than can a doctor in solo or small group practice.

We also know that organizations can integrate the care teams and care processes for the benefit of patients. They also can provide the support and the capital and be accountable for the care that is provided within the organization. The Mayo Clinic, founded in the late 1800s, has done this for more than a century. Large medical organizations like the Cleveland Clinic, the Oschner Clinic, and the Virginia Mason Clinic carry out these functions and have provided excellent care to patients for several decades. Specialty organizations such as the Sloan Kettering Cancer Center, the MD Anderson Cancer Center, the Fred Hutchinson Cancer Center, and the National Jewish Hospital for Children provide integrated care and support within certain disease categories. Group Health Cooperative, HealthPartners, Harvard Pilgrim, Kaiser Permanente, Henry Ford Health System, and other fully integrated medical-care financing and delivery systems have demonstrated that comprehensive and superior care and excellent organizations go hand in hand. Intermountain Health Care and the Lovelace Clinic in New Mexico have effectively blended excellent medical care with strong organizations. The most effective of these organizations have established close ties to the communities they serve in order to enhance care for their patients and provide improved protections for the members of those communities.

The model, then, is far better for us as patients than what most of us have experienced throughout the twentieth century. But can it do what the traditional craft-based medical-delivery model has been unable to do? That is, can it respond to the major challenges that medicine faces now and in the future? Those challenges, discussed in detail in chapter 2, are:

- The changing expectations of patients

- The expanding pace and scope of discovery in medical science and technology

- The increasing number of Americans with chronic illnesses

- The growing complexity of medical care

- The increasing demand for transparency

- The nation's growing diversity

- The external threats to our health from bioterrorism, imported disease, and environmental hazards

Helping the patient become a partner in the care process, and providing the resources and time to address the patient's questions and needs, are important elements of the model. The availability of several professionals on the team increases the range of ideas and experiences on which the patient can draw and the opportunities to establish a healing relationship. This support also reduces the burden on the physician to try to do it all. The care team, nested in a larger organization, can assemble the resources and draw on support systems that bring the expanding medical science and technologies to each patient. This combination also facilitates the process of separating the useful from the irrelevant and incorporating the acceptable new practices and technologies into the care process. As we have seen, the model is drawn from the successful experiences of others in treating chronic illness.

The model also brings together the fragmented pieces of medical care and adds important new elements: communications and information systems, care process design, continuous quality improvement, and administrative support. This level of coordination reduces complexity. The organization provides heft and resources to deal with the outside forces that impact on medical care: legal and regulatory bodies and actions; payment systems; and the growing demand for transparency and data on performance. As noted, the care team itself broadens the range of professionals who can interact with patients from different backgrounds. Although more responsiveness to diverse patients is not guaranteed by the model, it is possible when the team is constructed with this goal in mind. The organization has the resources to assemble the professionals, support staff, and support systems to address this challenge. Similarly, the organization can assemble staff and resources to build and maintain the linkages between the care teams and the community.

## Alternatives

Other options have been suggested. One, for example, is to return to the mythical family physician. The idea is that a trained family physician knows enough to deal with routine illnesses and understands when he is out of his depth and needs to refer the patient to a specialist. The family physician is a coordinator of care, prepared to deal with the "whole" person and family, trained in patient counseling and education, and able to knit together what specialists provide. The limitations of this approach are several. It still relies on the physician as the caregiver instead of broadening the range of skills and experiences for the patient. The problems of time and resources remain. For routine illnesses, this is not an issue. But as illnesses grow complex, care is compromised. Furthermore, for these more serious conditions, the family physician must rely on other specialists. Without integration and coordination, common medical records, advanced communications systems, and the like, this option perpetuates, even adds to, the fragmentation and lack of coordination in the care process as the patient moves from doctor to doctor. There is nothing wrong with the family physician model as long as the physician is part of a care team and an organization that can integrate and support the care processes for the patient.

Another option is to expand the primary-care capabilities of the nation. Today only 20 to 30 percent of physicians in practice are primary-care specialists: family practice, internal medicine, general pediatrics, and general obstetrics and gynecology. Moreover, the number of medical students choosing to train in these specialties has declined steadily throughout the past decade. Patients would be better served with a higher proportion of primary-care physicians in the physician pool. Once again, though, the addition of these resources, perhaps necessary, is hardly sufficient. More than physicians are required to meet the challenges medicine faces.

Another suggestion for dealing with the way we get our care (as opposed to the way it is paid for) is to nationalize the entire medical-care delivery system, bringing it under public control like Great Britain's National Health Service. Even the casual observer of the British system, however, can see that the physician-craftsman model predominates, leaving care every bit as fragmented and disorganized as in the United States. In the case of medical-care delivery, private or public ownership is not the most important issue to address. Nor will changing the financing of care address the underlying delivery-system shortcomings. The matter of financial equity, of assuring that citizens of the United States have adequate medical-care insurance coverage, is vitally important. Our nation's inability to resolve this problem is unconscionable. But if, by waving a wand, we could create universal coverage, the nation's delivery system would remain unable to meet the challenges it now faces.

## Unanswered Questions

As encouraging as the experiences are, and as suggestive as the research findings might be, important work remains if we are to build effective, care team–based, integrated delivery models. Several issues deserve mention.

To begin, there is much more to learn about how to achieve and sustain the kind of primary relationship with a physician that most patients seek while supporting the other important relationships that occur between the patient and the team members. Similarly, while individual physicians in small or solo practices struggle to obtain the resources and support they need to practice competent medicine, medical organizations have struggled to create the intimacy and personal responsiveness that are required for healing and caring. Law and culture reinforce physician leadership in delivering medical care, yet care teams are by design nonhierarchical. Although successful teams have found ways to resolve this conflict, more work is required, and additional legal and regulatory tests must occur before a common understanding emerges in law and practice. To practice medicine today requires excellent communications and information systems; integrated-care processes for the benefit of the patient also depend on this support. Once again, law, regulation, and culture have not caught up with the technology: Issues of privacy, access to one's medical records, installation and maintenance costs, and liability will be important to resolve as the nation moves toward the integrated model of care.

There is also the matter of feasibility. Patients continue to seek the mythical Dr. Welby. Care teams are the exception in medicine. Physicians are firmly entrenched in their comfortable, respectable, and well-paid craftsmen roles; many medical professionals are, too. Few organizations exist to knit care together for patients; most that do, such as hospital companies, nursing-home operators, laboratories, and home health agencies, focus on one or two pieces of the puzzle. They are not organized to integrate care for patients across multiple physicians, professionals, and institutions. Information technology, the backbone for care teams and care integration, has been adopted slowly, especially in clinical practice; medicine remains one of the last sectors to enter the digital age when it comes to medical information, knowledge management, and care process management. Communications systems are relatively primitive as well. Medical schools continue to train physicians to be independent professionals with little or no experience working collaboratively in care teams, either with other medical professionals or with patients.

Getting there is the biggest challenge we face.

# 8

# GETTING THERE

IN THE OLD comedy album *Bert and I,* an exchange occurs between a city slicker and a farmer from Maine. The slicker asks the farmer how to get from where he is now to a town some distance away. After struggling through several possibilities that don't work, the farmer concludes, "Well, Mister, you just can't get there from here."

One is tempted to reach the same conclusion about getting from where we are today in medicine to the medical-care system we need. Changes take place so slowly, with such drama and anger, that it often feels that we just can't get there from here. Certainly, medicine will continue to evolve. But it will not and cannot change rapidly enough on its own. For patients, this means that the well-documented problems in care will continue to grow unless new forces are brought to bear on the system itself.

Let's first examine why the changes cannot occur fast enough or far enough from within the current system. Then we will turn to four groups that, acting together, can accelerate the changes and by so doing increase the likelihood we will get there from here.

# The Constraints

## Physicians

Physicians, as well as other medical professionals and the institutions of medical-care delivery, are trapped in a tight, nearly impenetrable cocoon of culture, habit, law, payment systems, myth, and self-interest. Socialized from the day they enter medical school to operate as highly independent professionals, most physicians lack the training and perspective to work with other medical professionals in collegial and interdependent relationships. As Paul Starr pointed out in his classic book, *The Transformation of American Medicine: The Rise of a Sovereign Profession,* physicians have steadily asserted in law and culture their right to lead, decide, and supervise others. Care teams require collaboration and a democratic spirit. The clinical problem, patient preferences, and abilities of the team members, rather than status or tradition, determine who leads and decides.

When physicians enter practice, they bring their medical cookbooks with them—the approaches, decision rules, and treatments learned in training. They organize their practices based on what they know and have experienced. After that, the demands and economics of practice take over. Time is limited, practice patterns become habits, and learning slows. There is an old saying in medicine: "You're never smarter than the day you finish residency." Of course, that's not true. Experience is a great teacher, especially for physicians. The fact remains, though, that once a physician establishes his practice, habits are formed that are hard to change. Finding and incorporating new approaches into one's practice is a major challenge, and the opportunities for learning become harder and harder to fit into the daily routine.

Apart from the constraints that bind them to their current way of practicing, physicians and other medical professionals have little motivation to change. It isn't in their interest. Physicians, after all, are at the top of the pecking order in medicine, hold a revered place in our society, and make a good living to boot. Patients seek their help and want what they offer. The rewards of their profession, both psychological and economic, are significant in spite of the frustrations of daily practice. Other medical professionals do well, too. They are often organized into professional groups, unions, or advocacy organizations, so they have a voice in the way they are paid and their conditions of work, and they can often influence legislation and regulations to their advantage.

## Popular Myths

Two important myths reinforce the status quo as well. As mentioned in chapter 2, the doctor of our imagination has been shaped by the tempting notion of the fabled family doctor embodied in once-popular television shows like *Marcus Welby, M.D., Young Doctor Kildare,* and *Ben Casey, M.D.* The mythical physician on these shows was independent and combined remarkable gentleness, brilliant diagnostic skills, infinite patience, uncanny intuition, and attractive, plainspoken human insights to solve problem after difficult problem for his always grateful patients. He was the master of medical science and the fierce protector of his patients. Of course, no physician can be so accomplished today, but the myth persists. We expect our doctor to make us well or to ensure that other physicians act in our best interests when he refers us to a specialist. We expect him, and all the physicians with whom we interact, to be well trained, up to date, interested in us, and infallible as we move from one to another in the course of getting care. There is little room in this myth for care by a team of professionals, or for organizations that make care possible.

This isn't the only myth at work in our culture. Spend an evening in front of the television set and count the advertisements for new medicines that you see. Look at the range of illnesses and symptoms the new wonder drugs are supposed to help. In one evening, I saw slick, heart-tugging advertisements for medications to relieve heartburn, control allergies, relieve asthma, lower cholesterol, calm social anxiety, combat heart disease, relax overactive bladders, relieve tired eyes, convert gray hair to brown, take the pain out of osteoarthritis, enhance sexual performance, and help aging bones get stronger. Or glance through a newspaper or magazine or watch the evening news. You'll be surprised at how often some new cure or medical advance is touted. Have a bad hip? Replace it. A bad heart? Operate on it or put in a better one. Tear up your knee playing tennis? Arthroscopic surgery is for you. Overweight? Eat a sub sandwich. Cataracts? Wait until you try the latest intraocular lenses. Got a question or a symptom? Talk to your doctor. Always. Go see your doctor to get the help you need. This is the myth of the magic bullet. With the right doctor, the right drug, the right hospital, or the right surgery, everything can be cured. Sometimes there really are magic bullets. We see our doctor, get a prescription or a surgery, and presto, we're cured. But for most illnesses, especially complex or chronic ones, the care goes on for a long time and the disease may never be cured.

Together, these two myths—the physician of our dreams, and the magic bullet that cures—shape our expectations for medicine. Those with complex illnesses and chronic conditions might find one mythical physician if they're fortunate, but not the several they'll need. Nor will they find an easy cure. Ask anyone who has spent months in physical rehabilitation after knee surgery, or a lifetime managing diabetes. They know better.

## The Lack of Organizations and Systems

Author J. D. Kleinke wrote, in *The Oxymoron: The Myth of the U.S. Healthcare System,* that there is little "system" in the medical-care system. Centers of excellence exist throughout the country, as noted earlier. Although some integrate care to some degree, interact with the communities they serve, and provide critical infrastructure on which to build the delivery system of the future, they operate independently of one another. Of course, they talk and share ideas and even meet periodically. But they do not build systems together, hire and train people together, or invest together in the way organizations that operate at scale do. And scale, heft, resources, and systems are precisely what is needed to improve medical delivery. Moreover, organizations, at least the good ones, provide the focus and resources for making the changes. Their leaders maintain a clear view of the destination when everyone else is busy responding to daily demands. They, and the organizations they represent, help people elevate themselves out of that daily grind to see and shape the future.

Organizations and systems, however, are anathema to many physicians. And despite evidence to the contrary, many patients believe that organizations and systems mean loss of the personal and intimate relationships they seek from their professional caregivers. So we face a dilemma. Not only are there few organizations and limited systems on which to build the delivery system of the future, but those who must use them do not want them and are unlikely to participate enthusiastically in their creation. Innovations will continue to come from the professionals and institutions of medicine, and these will be shared across medicine by organizations like the Institute for Healthcare Improvement, the Improving Chronic Illness Care initiative, and HRET. But to accelerate the changes to transform the medical-care delivery system will require the force of others outside medicine.

## Four Groups That Must Drive the Changes in Medicine

Four groups have the potential to bring significant leverage to a reluctant delivery system in order to speed the changes medicine requires. Acting independently, they are unlikely to have much impact on an enterprise as large as medical care. But together, applying their collective strength, they could force the ponderous behemoth into something faster than a plodding, resistant walk.

- *Payers,* the combination of employers, union trusts, and governments at all levels, provide about 85 percent of the funds that pay for medical care today. The rest is provided by individual patients and families.

- *Intermediaries,* the health plans, health-insurance companies, and administrative services, handle most of the funds, pay the providers, and design the medical benefits and delivery choices from which medical consumers choose.

- *State and federal governments* buy care, in fact a lot of it. Some researchers estimate that more than half the funds flowing into the medical-care system come from government in one form or another. Governments also set and enforce the rules. They invest in infrastructure, research, and development. They educate. And sometimes they even lead.

- *Medical consumers,* those who select insurance coverage for themselves and their dependents, use medical-care services, and pay some portion of the costs of care, are the linchpin. The dollars that pay doctors, medical professionals, and medical institutions follow the consumers into the delivery system. In groups of one sort or another, they demand that certain protections, benefits, and services are provided to them. Individually, they choose among benefit alternatives and delivery systems when they select coverage for a given period. When they are sick, they choose which care providers to go to, what advice to follow, what medications to take, and what treatments to select.

The interests of the four groups are often distinct, sometimes conflicting. Patients want employers to pay for broad coverage and a wide range of choices; employers want to control their costs; intermediaries want to manage their risks so they can earn a profit; and governments have limited funds and want to avoid significant social or political instability. But all four groups share a common interest in making sure the delivery system is ready for us when we need it, regardless of where we sit today. We will all be patients at some time in our lives. So will our parents and our children. We share an interest in making sure care is affordable now and in the future. These common concerns, not our differences, are the interests we can build on to create an agenda for change.

To act effectively, the leverage of the four groups must be used fully and aggressively. There are several opportunities to do so.

## Health Benefits

The design of health benefits determines who pays and what care is paid for. Significant copayments and deductibles for patients mean that the patient may delay or avoid care that can help. Nonexistent or negligible payments may lead patients to be less discriminating in what they seek and demand more services than they need. When the cost of coverage becomes too high, payers may reduce benefits, shift costs, or stop offering coverage to their employees and beneficiaries. To encourage the formation of care team–based, integrated medical-delivery solutions, benefits can be designed to encourage integrated care from care-team members for patients with complex and chronic conditions and to minimize barriers for early diagnosis, prevention, and health maintenance. Coverage for other support services in the community can be covered as well.

## Medical-Delivery Options

The second opportunity lies with the medical-delivery choices made available to employees and beneficiaries by payers and intermediaries. One way to exercise leverage is to ensure that every employee and beneficiary has a choice of at least one care team–based, integrated medical-care option in regions and cities where this option exists. Over time, as more of these solutions become available, it may be in the best interests of payers and consumers to include only integrated solutions in the offerings available. After all, the evidence clearly shows that the care is superior and the costs more affordable than in the fragmented, mom-and-pop alternative.

## Incentives

Incentives can be used to exert leverage at several levels. The share the employer contributes to pay for employee medical-insurance coverage can be greater for more comprehensive benefits and integrated solutions. This makes it advantageous to the medical consumer to choose these options over less structured alternatives. The amount patients pay when they utilize services in an integrated setting also can be lower. Payers like the Leapfrog Group are exploring how to reward medical-care organizations that incorporate the best practices to improve patient safety. Leading American companies carefully assess medical-care quality and affordability and provide their employees with larger contributions when they choose the best delivery options. Medical consumers can exert pressure as well by leaving practices that do not include care teams and are not part of integrated organizations.

## Data

A common saying in American industry is that "you manage what you measure." Data, especially measurements of performance, can reveal how systems compare and how fast they are improving, and whether care teams are in place and how well they are doing. We can track how long it takes a patient to get from the initial symptom of an illness to appropriate treatment and return to normal life. Frequency of complications, visits to the emergency room, and hospitalization suggest how well a medical-care system integrates and provides comprehensive, up-to-date care for patients.

## Education

With the results of research comparing the performance of different doctors, teams, and institutions, we can educate ourselves about the best solutions. This is a shared responsibility among the four groups, as each has a slightly different window into medical care and a different set of concerns. To make the required changes, we will have to replace the old myths about physicians and medical care with new stories and solutions, and then insist that the solutions we choose are consistent with them. We can expect those within medicine to resist. And their most powerful avenue for doing so will be to play on our fears and reinforce those old myths. In part, this is what created the backlash against managed care. Restricted choices upset consumers, to be sure. But contributing to the anger that consumers developed against managed care (anyone who heard a movie audience respond to the comment about HMOs by actress Helen Hunt in the movie *As Good As It Gets* understands how angry medical consumers are) were the physicians, who shared their concerns openly with their patients. Information and education are antidotes for this resistance.

## Oversight

The four groups can build on efforts already under way to provide greater oversight of medical care. The opportunities already exist: The National Quality Forum, the National Committee for Quality Assurance, and the Foundation for Accountability are three of many organizations. The more active payers, insurers, and government and medical consumers are in shaping these institutions, the greater the leverage in terms of the directions in which the medical-care system moves. Similarly, coalitions specific to each group can work collaboratively to pursue a common agenda. There is strength in numbers, especially when dealing with something as large and immovable as medical care.

## Coalitions

Coalitions that cross the four groups are also valuable. It is in the interest of the American Nurses Association to promote care teams and enhance patient care through greater integration. The American Hospital Association may also be an ally in this endeavor. Other professional associations may choose to join as well. Emerging coalitions like the Alliance for Health Reform and the National Coalition on Health Care, both headquartered in Washington, D.C., have the potential to exercise considerable influence on public policy development. Until the opportunities are explored, we won't know. Whatever the outcome, it is clear that if the four groups are joined by influential organizations within medicine, the leverage can increase dramatically.

The work that remains is to identify the specific levers each group can and will pull, separately and together, to create the greatest pressure on the medical-care system. It won't be easy. The groups themselves are still fragmented, and efforts to bring them together have met with mixed success. Coalitions that reach across the groups and the medical-care system have struggled as well. Inertia within medicine is powerful; resistance to change is likely to be fierce.

Accelerating the changes requires that the four groups develop a common understanding of why the medical-care system doesn't work now and what damage occurs as a result. The change will require a sense of how medicine is changing already, the forces driving those changes, and an understanding of where the resistance to change lies. It means understanding where the leverage is and how best to exert it. And finally, it requires a shared goal, a well-defined vision of what the system needs to become to meet the challenges medicine faces.

One might ask why greater speed and effort is necessary if we will get there eventually anyway. After all, change of this magnitude promises to be disruptive and unpleasant, and people's livelihoods will be affected. The answer, I believe, is that the stakes are too high not to. If the medical system is allowed to change at the pace of the past fifty years, more than 2 million people are likely to die at its hands in the next ten years. They will be our parents, our children, and some of us. For every person who dies, many more will suffer unnecessary harm. In that same period, most American families will have distressing problems in obtaining care for their parents, their children, and themselves, especially when they have complex illnesses or chronic conditions, or if they speak English poorly or have roots in cultures that are different from the mainstream. And medical care will consume more than $10 trillion with only modest improvements.

We cannot lose our friends and our families this way, especially when the path to far better medical care is so clearly marked, and when the opportunity to shape the future is so clearly understood. Nor can we afford to squander our resources this way, especially knowing that doing so produces such marginal benefits and can cause so much pain. We understand where we need to go, and we know that if we fail to act, the challenges facing medicine will place greater stress on a system that is already overwhelmed. We know that the most fundamental requirement is to create care teams in which patients are partners with their physicians and medical professionals in making decisions and managing their care. We know that organizations must integrate care teams and provide the experts and support systems to meet patient needs and expectations in the face of these challenges. And we know that care must include critical resources from the community to be most effective, especially for those whose illnesses disrupt their lives and livelihoods. We know that only when medical professionals work within systems like these can they help us realize the full benefits of the remarkable promise of modern medicine to heal us and help us.

# 9

# REFLECTIONS:
# REBECCA'S MOTHER LOOKS BACK

*Patients and their families benefit most from a team-based approach to medical care; in that light, we now turn back to Rebecca to hear, from her mother's perspective, how the model impacts Rebecca and her family.*

IT'S BEEN EIGHT years now since we first learned Rebecca had asthma. It's hard to believe what she has been through; what we've all been through. Hospitals, emergency rooms, the medicines, shots. All those doctors and nurses we've seen, and the other medical people, too. It's sure changed the way I think about medicine.

Like doctors. I always went to the doctor to find out what was wrong and get medicines or surgery. If it didn't work the first time, I kept going back until the doctor figured out what was going on. It was comforting to turn things over to them and get fixed. That used to work for the kids, too, probably because they were never very sick. So we assumed the same thing would happen with Rebecca. We thought Dr. Landers would give her

163

prescriptions, help her when she had an emergency, and refer her to other doctors when he needed to. That was pretty much what happened, and Rebecca didn't do too well.

Dr. Wilkensen, Dr. Foxton, and their team had a different approach. They told us that we would work together with them to take care of Rebecca. At first it didn't seem right. I wanted them to tell us what to do, find the right treatments, and make Rebecca okay. I felt pretty helpless. But they helped us learn what to do. So did the parent group. We got so we could handle a lot of the decisions we used to depend on Dr. Landers to make. When we didn't know what to do, someone was always there to help.

When you think about it, being partners with the doctors and the team makes a lot of sense. We're with Rebecca all the time. They only see her a few times a year. We're there at night when she starts to wheeze and needs extra treatments. We give her the medicines and make sure she isn't around things that trigger her attacks. She does a lot of it, too. Every day. No one knows what's going on with her lungs better than she does, especially as she gets older. Now she does most of what she has to do without being reminded. Oh sure, she forgets and wants to be a little girl and sometimes she complains about having "dumb asthma" and all the medicines. But she gets over it pretty quickly.

There were times I wanted the doctors to take over when the responsibilities got to be too much. We'd get careless, forget to do the peak flow meter, or be late with the inhaler or something. Not get right on things when Rebecca had a cold. That's when she would start to get sick. After a while, taking care of Rebecca got to be second nature and we didn't think about it very much. Still, I keep wishing someone else could solve the problem for us, but I guess that isn't going to happen.

When I first heard about the asthma team, I was really uncomfortable. Everyone I know has a doctor and wants their own physician. The team idea was confusing. There were too many people involved; it was too much like a committee. I had to get to know Dr. Wilkensen and Dr. Foxton, figure out how to make appointments and fill prescriptions and get lab and X-ray work. That was a lot. On top of it, they wanted us to work with a bunch of people who weren't doctors. I found out pretty quickly, though, that each of them could help us with Rebecca. They had a lot of important information to pass along and ideas that added to what Dr. Wilkensen and Dr. Foxton could tell us.

My biggest concern was that no one was in charge and that we'd get conflicting advice, like we did when Dr. Landers and all the others were taking care of Rebecca. But this didn't happen. Everyone uses the same medical record, and they all talk with each other and follow the same basic treatment approach. I guess Dr. Foxton is in charge, but it never really comes up. They all work together so well, it's just not an issue anymore.

One advantage I've found with the team is that we have someone to talk to besides the doctor when problems come up. Dr. Foxton is always busy. So is Dr. Wilkensen, our pediatrician. The others have more time. I could always talk with Louise Morrison, the nurse care manager. John really liked Dr. Foxton; they had a good relationship. Rebecca talked with everyone, but her favorite, if she really needed some advice, was Louise or Ercilia, the home visit nurse. We could see Dr. Foxton, Dr. Wilkensen, or one of their partners when we really needed to. I've developed a good relationship with Dr. Wilkensen. I trust her and know she'll either take care of the children or get them to the people who can. There are some things only a doctor knows about—the real ins and outs of asthma, the special treatments, the signs of serious complications—things like that. But there are a lot of things Dr. Wilkensen and Dr. Foxton don't have time to do, or that the other team members know more about. So it seems to me that we're getting the best of both worlds.

There were times when I wanted to dump the team. Not because I didn't like everyone. I just wanted everything to be simple—see the doctor, get a few medicines, and make Rebecca better. But every time we'd get discouraged, someone on the team was there for us, encouraging us, giving us new ways to think about things, letting us ventilate. I know asthma isn't simple, as much as I wish it were. If you're going to keep the condition from getting out of hand, you've got to stay on it every day, like washing the dishes or picking up after yourself. And you need a lot of help to do that. The team is always there, at least someone, and if that person doesn't know the answer, she can always find someone else who does.

That's another big change for me. I realize now there is no magic bullet for asthma. I used to read about some new drug or see it advertised on television, and my hopes would go up. It always sounds so good, as though the scientists have found the perfect treatment. I guess it was natural of me to have high hopes. It would be a lot easier if we could find some wonder drug that took care of it once and for all. But the truth is, we're taking care of our child who has a condition that no one can cure, and it won't go away. All we can do is try to control it and keep it from getting bad the way it used to. It's a lot of work, that's what it is; a lot of work and worry. I wish there were a cure. What mother wouldn't? I hate that Rebecca always has to think about her asthma. But I'm not going to hold my breath. If something comes along that takes care of asthma for good, great. Meanwhile, we want Rebecca's life to be as close to normal as possible.

One good thing about learning to care for Rebecca is that we don't have to go to the doctor or the emergency room all the time. I used to feel like we were imposing on the doctors and the nurses, like it was our fault we had to bring Rebecca in to see them. Once we got the care Rebecca needed—what we should have been getting all along—we didn't have to come in very often, except for checkups. It's a pain to go to the doctor. I have to figure out what to do with the kids, and my business partner has to cover the store for me. When we had to go to the emergency room at night like we used to, John and I always had to find a neighbor to stay at the house. Then we were exhausted the next day. It's a lot better to figure out what to do at home, or call someone for help when you need it. As much as I like Dr. Wilkensen and Dr. Foxton and the rest of the team, I'd just as soon never have to see them again. I'm joking. I don't really mind, because they need to keep track of how Rebecca's doing. But in a way I mean it. Every visit I avoid, every trip to the hospital that John and I don't have to make with Rebecca, is better for her and us. I want them to be there if we need them, but if I could get by going in to see Dr. Wilkensen or Dr. Foxton and the rest of the team once a year, I'd be happy.

One thing that bothered me at first was the computer on the doctor's desk. Dr. Wilkensen had all our records on her computer; so did Dr. Foxton and the rest of the team. All our information was right there. I didn't like it. It seemed so cold and impersonal, and I worried that any half-sophisticated hacker could get into the file and find out whatever they wanted about our family. Then I thought about how Dr. Landers kept his records. In a written chart. All those pages he had to read through to find out what was going on with Rebecca. No wonder he couldn't keep track of things. Besides, the records were always lying around somewhere in the office, so that the office staff could read anything they wanted to. I know they're supposed to keep things confidential, but it's human nature to gossip a little. And then I thought about the information the doctors have to keep up with. Dr. Wilkensen and Dr. Foxton have the help built right into their computers. I know, because sometimes we'll sit side by side at the computer reviewing how Rebecca's doing. Dr. Wilkensen showed me how it works; because of the computer, she doesn't have to rely on her memory so much and can have more time to answer our questions. I know what it's like to try to keep things like that straight. We even get confused sometimes with Rebecca's care, forgetting which medicine she's on, or trying to remember how to use a medicine if we haven't needed it for a few weeks. At my shop, we couldn't keep track of prices and inventories without the computer. When I think about how much a doctor has to think about to take care of so many patients every day, I don't know how it can be done without the help of the computer.

When I thought about it this way, I realized the trade-off is worth it. I asked Dr. Wilkensen how easily someone could break into the computer, and she told me she'd worried about the same thing. So had the other doctors. So they tested the security system and believe it's a good one. Sure, someone who really wanted to could probably break in, I guess. But compared to Dr. Landers's records, the information in the computer is a lot more secure. And this way, everyone taking care of Rebecca has access to the same information, knows what the treatments are, sees when there have been complications, and uses the same approach to care. It makes a lot more sense.

The other thing about the computer is that it makes it easier to do studies to see how to improve things. Every now and again, we and the other parents would sit down with the team and go over what they'd learned. And they'd ask for our ideas about how to make things better. They were always looking for better ways to take care of the kids. And you could see how it worked. They'd change medications after their studies showed that the medication other researchers had found to be useful didn't work as well in their practice. Or they'd find new ways to teach us the skills we needed.

At one parent's meeting, Dr. Foxton and Paul Guzman, the pharmacist, showed us how they review the scientific studies to decide how to treat the children. I had no idea how many studies they have to go through. Each one is a little bit different, so the trick is to put the information together into something that makes sense. Dr. Foxton said that the science is always changing; their job is to take the best of it so that each child gets the benefit of what is most likely to help. He told us that when he was in private practice, he never had time or the help to do this, so he always had to rely on courses he took, or reading the journals when he had time, or the drug salesmen. Now people help him keep on top of the science, and they have the tools to pull it all together. Then it's built into the computer so he doesn't have to remember it all. That way, he can concentrate on the patient and the family.

That's another piece of the puzzle for me. I never realized how many people are needed to take care of Rebecca and kids like her. Besides Dr. Wilkensen and Dr. Foxton, and the asthma team, there are all sorts of other people and the computer systems and the pharmacies and all the rest behind the scenes. It's really complicated. I'm not a big fan of organizations. They always seem too big and bureaucratic and impersonal, and you have to fight your way through them to get what you need. I've felt that way at the health-care organization sometimes when I have to wait on hold for the phone to be answered, or when the computer system is down and no one knows us or can't find anything out about Rebecca. It doesn't happen often, but when it does, I don't like it. As long as we can work with Dr. Wilkensen and Dr. Foxton and the team, though, I try not to let the other things bother me. I don't think the team could do what they do for us without all that help anyway.

One last thing I sure have learned to appreciate is our insurance coverage. Before we had to pay a part of everything: prescriptions, emergency-room visits, doctor visits, hospital care, everything. It really added up, so sometimes, if things were tight, we'd think twice about going to see the doctor or getting a prescription filled. I can remember a couple of times when I held off taking Rebecca in to Dr. Landers's office because we had a lot of other bills that month. A lot of things weren't covered either. Like home visits or health education or pharmacy consultations. It was pretty expensive for us, and John and I both have good jobs. I don't know how some other people get by.

A friend of mine runs a small business and couldn't get medical insurance after her employee's husband had a heart attack and needed heart surgery. The rates went up so much the next year, she couldn't afford to keep the coverage. So she replaced the woman with someone younger to get the rates down far enough that she could get insurance for herself and her two children, since she's a single mom. Another friend had her baby prematurely. The baby was in neonatal intensive care for nearly three months and needs major surgery on her spine. My friend doesn't get insurance where she works. The only thing available is through some state insurance pool she can't afford. Now she doesn't know what to do. It doesn't seem fair. It isn't her fault the baby was born that way. And it isn't like that guy wanted a heart attack. Most of the time it seems like people who get sick don't have much warning. It just happens, like with cancer or diabetes, or a car accident that puts you in the hospital for lots of surgeries. John and I are really lucky to have health insurance, especially with so much covered. I don't know how people with serious conditions manage if they don't have what we do.

When I talk with my brother and his wife, or my friends, about what we've gone through with Rebecca, they have a hard time understanding. They're healthy and so are their children, so they can't appreciate how different it is when someone's really sick or needs the kind of care Rebecca does. They're always talking about how they would never go to a system like we do, how they want their own doctor and all that. I don't think we would have changed the way we think if Rebecca was like our other children. Dr. Landers was just fine for what they needed. But now I won't go back, not even for Michael and Jenny. I'm willing to put up with some of the little hassles and occasional snafus because we get so much more than we used to from Dr. Landers, even for our other kids. Same for John and me with our doctors. I'm even trying to get my mother to join up. She's getting older and has problems with her blood pressure, and I know that once she experiences what we have, she'll forget about her old doctor pretty quickly. Compared to what she's getting now, and the chaotic things we had to go through with Rebecca before, the care is just a lot better. It's as simple as that.

# ACKNOWLEDGMENTS

WRITING IS A SOLITARY act made possible by the support of many. I would like to express my appreciation to the following for the many ways in which they have inspired and assisted me. Colleagues on the Institute of Medicine committees on quality, safety, and medical-system reform provided many of the ideas from which this manuscript springs. Friends and colleagues from the Executive Sessions on Patient Safety at Harvard's Kennedy School introduced me to their work, provided the motivation to accelerate our efforts in Kaiser Permanente, and shared ideas that shaped my thinking thereafter. Penny Janeway, Michael Millensen, Nan Stone, and my daughter, Raisa Marshall, read early proposals from which this manuscript finally emerged. Their encouragement and suggestions helped immeasurably. Colleagues Ian Morrison, Steve Shortell, and Jack Shaw provided insights from their experiences organizing and completing the books they have written. Special friend Mary Reres did the same even as she battled her own illness.

Ned Barnholt, Maureen Bisignano, Phil Condit, John Hayward, George Isham, Brent James, Bob Master, Al Mulley, John Romer, Laurel Simmons, and Ana Lisa Sylvestre were generous with insights about their programs. They also took time to review and correct the sections of the book that refer to their work.* Harold Farber, a pediatric lung specialist at Kaiser Permanente, has collaborated with Michael Boyette to write an absorbing book about the KP asthma program for children, *Control Your Child's Asthma.* I have drawn heavily on their work to create the description of the care Rebecca and her family received from the asthma team.

I am indebted to Ed Wagner at Group Health for his work on care models for patients with chronic illness and his generosity in sharing his insights. The knowledgeable reader will see that I have expanded that model to cover a broader range of conditions and have added details to the discussions that Ed and his colleagues have carried out in print and presentations. Similarly, many of the ideas and recommendations in the three Institute of Medicine studies, *The Quality of Care in America, To Err Is Human,* and *Crossing the Quality Chasm,* have found their way into this book. Again, I have tried to build on them, adding from my experiences and from new evidence that has emerged since those studies were completed. I am particularly indebted to Bill Richardson, whose steady leadership and wisdom contributed so much to the work of the Institute Committee on Quality, and this work as well. His friendship has been an important gift. Colleagues from the Health Research and Educational Trust (HRET), especially Mary Pittman, HRET president, have stimulated my thinking about the many ways community resources can be linked to the medical-care system for the benefit of patients and communities alike. Don Berwick, president of the Institute for Healthcare Improvement, has been a friend and colleague for more than a decade. He generously shares stories and examples and provides leadership for all of us in medical care. Don's contributions to this book appear on virtually every page.

---

*John Hayward was unable to review the section on Peace Health due to other commitments. The description, therefore, is based only on notes from our conversation.

A project like this cannot happen without direct support from the teams who worked with me throughout its life.

The Board of Directors of Kaiser Foundation Health Plan and Hospitals—Dave Andrews, Tom Chapman, Dan Garcia, Henry Kaiser, Dorothy Mann, Dean Morton, Mary Reres, Bob Ridgley, and Chang Lin Tien—gave me the freedom and encouragement to pursue this project. Bill Foegge, who served as a board member for several years until other duties called him away, offered his counsel as well. The unwavering support of these special friends and colleagues has been a source of strength for which I am forever grateful. The Senior Leadership of Kaiser Foundation Health Plan and Hospitals managed our operations so that I could take time to participate in groups and discussions outside our organization, develop these ideas in print and speeches, and spend long hours writing. They and many Permanente physician-leaders played a critical part in shaping my thinking over the years. Partners and friends from the AFL-CIO worked with Kaiser Permanente leaders to find better ways to build an organization that draws on the talents of everyone, regardless of position. That effort is a blueprint for medical care that has informed my thinking throughout this book. Dick Butterfield, Beverly Hayon, Allan Mann, and Jean Tips gave me the courage to tell stories. Rafe Sagalyn helped focus the proposal, linked me to Perseus Publishing, provided encouragement and wisdom, and gently reminded me to meet deadlines. Marnie Cochran at Perseus and Katharine Duane provided careful editing, myriad suggestions, and helpful enthusiasm. Annie Burke, whose nickname remains within our family circle, was a willing researcher, finding sources I didn't know existed and never failing in her energy and intelligence.

My support staff were always there: Sharon Virgo kept day-to-day matters in hand when I was away; Patricia Florida produced draft after draft of the document; and Tanya Koodrin fielded calls from members. A special thanks goes to Joan Vallez

Simmons, my longtime secretary, who, with unfailing courtesy and grace, found new and creative ways to protect my time, arrange my schedule, field phone calls, send messages, and manage my office while I was hidden away in Oregon or California.

Above all, I am deeply grateful to my family. Our children, Raisa, Jennifer, Mackinnon, and Katharine, have been unwavering in their support and enthusiasm. My cousins Scott and Jennifer, and their brothers Mike and Blake, brought me into their parents' home when their father, Uncle Bill, was dying of cancer. Although the story of Bill and his wife, Mary Lou, is not included in this narrative, their experiences and spirits suffuse the entire book. My partner, Stephanie . . . what can I say? This book could not have been completed without your example, wisdom, humor, care, and love. No one could ask for more.

Whatever others have provided in the way of support, suggestions, ideas, and experiences, I alone am responsible for converting their contributions into this book.

# INDEX